Curriculum Map

Course	Level 1–7	Text Book
General Conversation	Essential English : Begin Again Pre Get Up to Speed 1~2 New Get Up to Speed 1 New Get Up to Speed 2 New Get Up to Speed 3 New Get Up to Speed 4 Daily Focused English 1 Daily Focused English 2	
Discussion	Active Discussion 1 Active Discussion 2 Dynamic Discussion Chicken Soup Course Dynamic Information & Digital Technology	
Business Conversation	Pre Business Basics 1 Pre Business Basics 2 Business Basics 1 Business Basics 2 Business Practice 1 Business Practice 2	
Global Biz Workshop	Effective Business Writing Skills (Workbook) Effective Presentation Skills (Workbook) Effective Negotiation Skills (Workbook) Cross-Cultural Training 1~2 (Workbook) Leadership Training Course (Workbook)	
Business Skills	Simple & Clear Technical Writing Skills Effective Business Writing Skills Effective Meeting Skills Business Communication (Negotiation) Effective Presentation Skills Marketing 1 Marketing 2 Management	
On the Job English	Human Resources Accounting and Finance Marketing and Sales Production Management Automotive Banking and Commerce Medical and Medicine Information Technology Construction Construction English in Use 1 ~ 4 Public Service English in Use	

※ This Curriculum Map illustrates the entire line-up of textbooks at CARROT HOUSE.

CARROT HOUSE
P.O.Box #2924, St. Marys, Ontario, Canada

Effective Business Writing

Printed : July 2019

Author : Carrot Language Lab

ISBN 978-89-97179-36-7

Printed and distributed in Korea
9th, 488m Gangnam St., Gangnam-gu,
Seoul 06210, Korea

Effective Business Writing Before you begin, take a minute to assess your writing style. You may discover that you know a lot more than you think, or you may discover specific areas where you need to improve. Either way, this exercise will help you assess your writing abillty.

Effective Business Writing

CARROT HOUSE

Introduction

CARROT House Methodology

Andragogical Approach & Productive English

The teaching of children (pedagogy) and adult learning (andragogy) are distinctively different. Pedagogy is akin to training and encourages convergent thinking and rote learning. It is compulsory, centered on the teacher and the imparting of information with minimal control by the learner. Andragogy, by contrast, is about education as freedom. It encourages divergent thinking and active learning. It is voluntary, learner oriented and opens up vistas for continuing learning. Adults need to feel independent and in control of their learning. Therefore, CARROT HOUSE curriculum is based on andragogy and is designed to encourage learners' participation and engagement by providing more task-based activities and opportunities to frequently interact in the classroom.

People want to achieve communicative competence when they learn other languages. English education in EFL environments has been rather focused on the receptive skills of English—listening and reading—which simply increases learners' knowledge about a language, not the competence of using it. If people are well equipped with productive skills—speaking and writing—they will be competent in English communication.

This is why CARROT HOUSE curriculum is designed to enhance learners' productive skills throughout the course. This andragogical approach of the CARROT HOUSE Curriculum, which focuses on productive English, will enable learners to achieve communication skills necessary for global competence. CARROT HOUSE's teaching philosophy and curriculum combine to provide a "Language for Success" for all learners.

Communicative Language Learning (CLL)

This communicative interaction, the essential component of language acquisition, does not occur in a typical, non-meaningful, fun-oriented conversation with native speakers. It occurs in a negotiated interaction through which a well-trained teacher provides the comprehensible input that is appropriate to the learners. The learners, at the same time, actively utilize the opportunities given to them by the teachers.

To this end, the Communicative Language Learning (CLL) method is employed in the field of Foreign Language Acquisition. The CLL method provides activities that are geared toward using language pragmatically, authentically and functionally with the intention of achieving meaningful purposes.

Course Objectives

This book, EFFECTIVE BUSINESS WRITING, is designed to teach learners the basics they need to become a better writer. The accompanying exercises will enhance learners' writing skills and are relevant to the practical demands of the business world. By the time learners complete this book, they will be better prepared to write a clear, concise business letter, memo, and report.

Unit Composition

Each unit of EFFECTIVE BUSINESS WRITING involves various sections as follow.

Questionnaire: This section provides a self-test for learners and an opportunity to experience writing issues in a personal way.

Input 1 and 2: Learners can acquire actual knowledge and information about business writing with these texts.

Exercises: Exercises provide learners with opportunities to check their understanding of writing. These exercises take the form of writing, revision, questionnaires, and discussions.

Business Writing Simulation: This section provides learners with opportunities to write various business documents based on Input 1 and 2.

Here are ten commandments for the best results in language learning:

1. Fear not.
2. Dive in.
3. Believe in yourself.
4. Seize the day.
5. Love thy neighbor.
6. Get the big picture.
7. Cope with the chaos.
8. Go with your hunches.
9. Learn from your mistakes.
10. Set your own goals.

CARROT HOUSE

Contents

Useful Expressions for Business Writing

in Different Situations

Useful Expressions for Business Writing
in Different Situations

Starting a Business Letter

- Introduce yourself

- Let me introduce myself.
- Allow me to introduce myself.
- Let me briefly introduce myself.
- I have been Director for two years.
- I am the head of the Marketing Department.
- I have been with this company for five years.

- State the purpose of your business letter

- In the January issue of *Financial World*, we saw the advertisement for your new products.
- Thank you for sending us the quote we requested last week for refrigerator no. TX-100E.
- I would like to report a regrettable experience I had in your restaurant.
- We are sorry that we are not able to fill your order.
- I am writing to let you know we have not received the items we ordered.
- This is to confirm your reservation you made for September 9th.

Ending Your Business Letter

- Thank you for your continuing support/patience.
- We look forward to receiving your comments on our proposal.
- If you have any questions about/regarding the products, please feel free to contact me.
- Please e-mail or fax your reply/order/quote/invoice.
- We would be happy to process your order.

Situation 1: Inquiries

[Basic Expressions]

- We are interested in ~.
- We would like to know ~.
- We would be grateful if you could let us know about ~.
- We would appreciate it if you could inform us about ~.

[Starting Your Letter]

- I found out about your company from *Business Week* of September 4th.
- I saw your advertisement in last week's *Time* magazine.
- I heard about your company from Mr. Anderson, one of your major clients.

[Inquiring]

- We are very interested in your graphics program and would appreciate receiving more information.
- I am writing this letter to request information about mass advertising.
- We would like to know more about your products.
- We would be very appreciative if you would provide us with your rates and any demographic information.
- I am writing to you because I have some questions about how you obtained patents for your products.
- We have attached a simplified financial statement form for your convenience.
- We would appreciate any information you can send to us.
- If you could send us information on your services, we would be grateful.
- Please fax us your wholesale price list along with the terms and conditions.
- I would like to get your latest catalog.

Situation 2: Requests

[Basic Expressions]

- We would like to make a request for ~.
- We are writing to ask for your cooperation in ~.
- Could you please ~?
- We would be grateful if you could ~.
- We would appreciate it if you could ~.
- I was wondering if you could help me.
- We are writing to ask if you can help us.
- I am (We are) writing to + verb.
- We are writing to enquire about ~.
- We are writing in connection with ~.
- We are interested in ~ and we would like to know ~.

[Starting Your Letter]

- I have just read the news on your networking tools that are scheduled to be released in December this year.
- I read/saw your advertisement on the woofers in the April 8th edition of *Engineering Monthly.*
- I have been given your name by Mr. David Han, Service Manager at ITM Corp.
- I saw your concept car demonstrated at the Seoul Motor Show.
- We have been manufacturing home medical appliances since 1950.
- We are a manufacturer specializing in electronic products.
- We currently import luxury goods mainly from Europe.

- We are retailers/wholesalers/importers of luxury goods.
- We would like to get in touch with suppliers in Europe.
- We are looking for distributors for our home theater devices to the Asian market.

[Requests]

- Please provide me with detailed information.
- Please send me further details.
- Please explain it in detail.
- I would like to request additional information on ~.
- I would appreciate it if you could send us further information on ~.
- If you have any other information available about ~, I would like to receive it.
- We would appreciate it if you could give us further details about ~.
- I would appreciate it if you would send us the quote at the following e-mail address: (tony@carrotkr.com).
- I would be grateful if you could provide us with the information by April 10th.
- We look forward to receiving your quote/prices/reply by the end of this month.
- A prompt reply would be appreciated.

[Feedback on Requests]

- ~ grant one's request / accept one's request
- comply with one's request
- We are able to ~. / We are happy to ~.
- We are pleased to tell you that ~.
- We are unable to ~.
- We regret to tell you that ~.
- ~ deny one's request/ refuse one's request
- I am afraid that I am unable to provide you with the information you need.
- I will get back to you with the information you need.
- I will be back in touch as soon as I find the information you need.
- I hope you find this information useful.
- I hope that this information is of help to you.
- We are enclosing a copy of our brochure.
- The sample will be sent to you today.
- For your review, we are attaching a copy of our catalog.
- You will receive our price list by November 30th.

Situation 3: Replies

[Basic Expressions]

- We have received your e-mail asking if ~.
- I am so delighted to hear from you.
- I am glad to have received your e-mail.
- Thank you for your recent e-mail concerning ~.
- Thank you for your inquiry about ~.
- I greatly appreciate ~.
- Thank you very much for ~.
- I wish to express my sincere appreciation for ~.

[Starting Your Letter]

- Today I received the quote I asked for last week.
- We are pleased to receive the information we requested on April 30th.
- Thank you for your inquiry on May 5th, expressing interest in our program.
- It gave us great pleasure to receive your order of September 27th.
- Thank you for your prompt response to my e-mail.
- Thank you for your quick reply.
- Thank you for getting back to me so quickly.

[Completing Your Letter]

- I would be happy to provide any further information you may need to place an order.
- If you need further details on our products, please contact us.
- If further information is required, please do not hesitate to contact us.
- I hope this will answer your question.
- Please let us have your order as soon as possible.
- Please do not hesitate to ask any questions concerning the product.
- I will be happy to answer any other questions you may have.
- If you have more questions or concerns, please feel free to contact me.
- If you need further information, please contact us at 245-5789.

Situation 4: Complaints and Adjustments

[Starting Your Letter]

- I am writing to express my extreme dissatisfaction about your service.
- I would like to bring to your attention a rather embarrassing situation I recently had.
- I am reporting an unpleasant encounter I had in one of your branches.
- I have some complaints to make about your service.
- We regret to inform you that your shipment of EXZ-8790 devices arrived today in unsatisfactory condition.
- We received the goods on January 15 with the following devices damaged.
- We found only 90 pieces in the carton although we ordered 100 pieces.

[Suggestions]

- If you cannot supply us with the products, please provide us with an explanation.
- Would you send us the missing manual by next week?
- If a satisfactory solution is not offered by November 5th, we will cancel our order.
- We want a refund immediately.
- The badly damaged items need to be replaced.
- Please let us know what compensation is available to us.
- The most satisfactory solution for us would be for you to give us a refund for the stolen items.
- I ask that the error be corrected immediately.
- I hope you will correct the problem immediately.
- I would appreciate your cooperation in immediately correcting this error.

Useful Expressions for Business Writing
in Different Situations

[Asking for an Immediate Action]

- Please take immediate action to settle this matter.
- Please investigate this matter thoroughly as soon as possible.
- Please look into the matter immediately.
- Please check the case promptly.

[Completing Your Letter]

- If a satisfactory solution is not offered by tomorrow, we will cancel our account with your firm.
- Unless we receive our order by March 12th, we will have to cancel it.
- If the goods do not arrive within a week, we will be forced to cancel the order.
- We are expecting you to resolve this problem so we can maintain this relationship.
- Thank you for your cooperation in this matter.
- We would appreciate it if you could promptly resolve this problem.
- I expect to hear from you by Monday.
- I need to know your answer by Friday.

Situation 5: Letters of Apology

[Basic Expressions]

- We are deeply sorry for ~.
- We sincerely apologize for ~.
- I can assure you that this will not happen again.
- Please let me know if there is anything I can do to help.
- Please accept our apologies once again.
- With apologies once again, ~.

[Starting Your Letter]

- Thank you for bringing the error to our attention.
- We are embarrassed to have made a mistake.
- I am very sorry about the mistake and I am grateful that you pointed it out.

[Apologizing]

- Thank you for your letter of August 13th regarding the poor service in our delivery department.
- We appreciate your letter of December 1st, expressing your unhappiness with the damaged DVD players.
- We are sorry to learn that the textile goods you purchased from us were lost at our warehouse.
- We apologize for the disappointment you have had with the shoes you ordered.
- We apologize for the inconvenience.
- Please accept our sincerest apologies for ~.
- We fully understand your frustration about the problem.
- I apologize for my late reply.
- I am so sorry that I could not get back to you earlier.
- I would like to apologize for the delay in replying to your e-mail.
- Please forgive me for not writing earlier.
- I am sorry for any inconvenience this has caused you.
- We hope that this has not caused you any inconvenience.

[Making a Suggestion]

- We have arranged to ship the right product.
- We are sending another cutter to you and it is scheduled to arrive at your warehouse next weekend.
- If you send the damaged set of climbing equipment back to us, we will replace it.
- We shipped you a replacement on February 8th.

[Completing Your Letter]

- We promise to do everything possible to prevent such a mistake.
- We hope that we can continue serving you in the future.
- Thank you again for bringing this matter to our attention. We look forward to continuing a good relationship.
- I hope this arrangement is satisfactory to you.
- We hope that this will be a satisfactory solution.
- I hope this will compensate for the trouble we have caused you.

Situation 6: Explaining

[Basic Expressions]

- This is due to a problem with our suppliers.
- We hope this e-mail has clarified the issue.
- I hope you understand that it is not our fault.
- We do not believe the responsibility lies with us.
- This is due to circumstances beyond our control.

[Bring up a Subject]

- I am afraid I have some bad news.
- I am sorry to inform you that ~.
- There has been a problem ~.
- We regret to advise you that ~.
- It is unfortunate that ~.
- We are sorry to hear that you are displeased with our products.

[Expressing Sympathy]

- I was concerned to learn that you have experienced an inconvenience in our agency.
- We are sorry that the optic analyzer you purchased from us is not working properly.
- I am afraid that the vegetables you received were completely damaged in transit.

[Explaining]

- As you can see from the attached document, the goods were in good condition when they left our port.
- With regret, we must inform you that the warranty does not cover the situation mentioned in your letter.
- Based on your description, we regret that there is little we can do about compensation.

[Making a Suggestion]

- We will be happy to assist you in another way.

- Although we believe we are not responsible for the damage, we would like to assist you in any way we can.
- If you have any questions, please contact us anytime.

Situation 7: Making Orders

[Expressions]

- I would like to order ~ from you.
- I would like to place an order for ~ with you.
- I would like to order the following items: ~.
- I am interesting in purchasing a large quantity of ~.
- Please send me the details of your products and prices.
- Could you please send me the details of your prices and models available?
- Thank you for your order of August 20th for 100 CD players, Model No. 1492X.
- We are pleased to confirm that we have booked your order for 100 boxes of red wine.
- We will confirm your order as follows: Item
  - No. 1492 X
  - Quantity : 100
  - Price : $2,000 ($20 per unit)

[Sellers]

- We are able to deliver the items you ordered by October 28th.
- Delivery is scheduled for November 22nd.
- We will make sure to deliver the products by December 23rd.
- We hope that this order will lead to further business in the future.
- We guarantee that this order and further orders will be given highest priority.
- We look forward to doing business with you again soon, and we will offer you an additional discount off your next order.
- I look forward to your confirmation.
- Please reconfirm the shipping date by e-mail.
- Looking forward to your reply.
- I look forward to hearing from you.
- I am looking forward to receiving your order (products).

[Negative Feedback]

- I am afraid I have to cancel the order.
- This is to cancel the order I placed on September 3rd.
- We would like to cancel our recent order for your product.
- We have reluctantly concluded that we will not be able to accept your order.
- We apologize for not being able to accept any orders until December.
- We are afraid that the digital cameras mentioned in your order are no longer available.
- We are sorry to inform you that the sewing machines (Model no. 289E) you ordered have been discontinued.
- We regret to inform you that the Macintosh cable modems, MDC-43651E, are no longer being manufactured.
- I hope you understand our position, and we hope that we can offer you substitutions that are satisfactory.
- If the substitution we have suggested meets your needs, please send us another order by e-mail.
- We look forward to offering you the best products and services again in the future.
- Please do not be reluctant to contact us whenever you need high quality products.

Situation 8: Collection Letters

[Urging to Pay]

- This is a reminder to inform you that our records show the payment for your October bill is late.
- This is to inform you that your account is past due. Please remit payment as soon as possible.
- This is just a reminder that your account has been overdue since November 14th.
- We would like to inform you that there is an outstanding balance of $5,000, which is now two months overdue.
- We sent you invoice no.244 last week, but we have received neither a reply from you nor a remittance.
- If you have any difficulties in making a payment in full, call us to make alternate arrangements.
- If you would like to make special arrangements for a settlement, do not hesitate to contact us at (02) 123-4567.
- To avoid affecting your credit standing, please remit your payment immediately.
- If we do not receive payment for invoice no.244 by November 30th, we will have to put this matter into the hands of a collection agency.
- If you do not offer a satisfactory response, we will have no choice but to file a suit against you to collect payment of invoice no.3445.
- If we do not hear from you by the end of the month, we will be forced to take legal action to recover the outstanding balance.

[Replies to Collection Letters]

- We are suffering from a temporary liquidity problem, so it is not possible for us to clear the account by the due date.
- Currently, we are having financial difficulties resulting from a long-lasting economic slump.
- Since our sales have dropped recently, we are having financial difficulties.
- Due to the devaluation of the won against the dollar, our profit has fallen dramatically.
- Would you allow us to postpone a settlement of the outstanding account?
- We would appreciate it if you would grant us an extension of three weeks to make the payment.
- In light of our long-standing relationship, please grant us an extension on our overdue account.
- We will arrange to make a payment by October 10th through Good Bank in settlement of invoice no.339-7.
- We are enclosing a check for $1,000 as a partial payment of invoice no.399-7.
- We are sending half of the amount now and will settle the remainder by paying in monthly installments.

Situation 9: Letters of Invitation

- You are cordially invited to a demonstration of our new line of products on Wednesday, April 3rd.
- We would like to invite a few of our best customers to a dinner banquet to be held on June 1st at the Grand-Sun Club.
- We sincerely hope you can join us for our company's celebration party.
- We will be holding a cocktail party for our 10th anniversary this weekend. Come join the celebration!

[Replies to Letters of Invitation]

- I will accept with pleasure your kind invitation to your demonstration of a new car on April 20th at 10:00 a.m.
- I would be delighted to attend the dinner banquet to celebrate winning the Good Design award.
- I would not miss your celebration for the world.
- I am looking forward to seeing you at the celebration.
- Thank you for the invitation, but I regret that I will not be able to attend due to a business trip that day.
- I would like to accept the invitation, but I have already made an appointment which cannot be cancelled.
- As much as I would like to attend your celebration, I have to be out of town on that day.
- Unfortunately, I must decline because of business I need to attend to.

Situation 10: Negotiating Conditions

[Sample Letter]

Dear Harry,
We have understood from your letter of October 20th that you would like us to give you a deeper discount.
We think the 10% discount you suggested to be rather high.
If you order 1,000 units or more, we can offer you a 10% discount.
We look forward to your prompt reply.

[Expressions]

- The details of the additional discount are explained in the enclosed brochure.
- Please inform us of your decision after you have had a chance to review this offer.
- The price we offered you is already the lowest we can offer.
- We are wondering if you can reduce the minimum order limit described in our contract.
- You qualify for a special discount on a family membership.

Situation 11: Absence Excuse Letters

[Expressions]

- I will be on vacation from October 16th to 18th.
- I will be taking a vacation next week.
- I will be on vacation for two weeks from tomorrow.
- I will be away from my desk.
- I will be away next week.
- I will be out of the office until Thursday.
- I am leaving town for a few days.
- I will be on a business trip for a week. I will be back to work on June 3.
- I will go to Canada on business next week. I will be back next month.
- Tomorrow is the 8th anniversary of the foundation of our company.
- I will be able to access my e-mail while I am away.
- I will be checking my e-mail though.
- Your e-mail will be forwarded.
- If it is urgent, please call me at this number, 010-4867-5486.
- If you need immediate assistance, I can be reached at the following e-mail address: ~.
- You can reach me on my cell if you need my assistance.
- Please contact Mr. Lee about the project while I am away.
- Please contact my colleague Tony Smith in the meantime.
- Jason Kim will handle your order and everything for the time being.
- Jenny Stewart is expected to replace me for a while.
- Julie Park will be responsible for you for now.
- Have a nice trip! / Have a safe journey! / Enjoy your trip!
- Have a great vacation. / Enjoy your vacation. / Have fun.
- Happy Lunar New Year! / Happy Chuseok! / Happy holidays!

Unit 1 Preparing to Write

Learning Objective:

After studying this unit, you should be able to....

- Understand when to use a comma(,), semicolon(;), colon(:), and apostrophe(').
- Write a business letter using the three steps of prewriting, writing, and revising.

Questionnaire : How well do you know your writing abilities?

Before you begin, take a minute to assess your writing style. You may discover that you know a lot more than you think, or you may discover specific areas where you need to improve. Either way, this exercise will help you assess your writing ability. Read each statement and mark the response that applies to you.

	Yes	No	I don't know
1. I keep my readers' perspective in mind when writing.			
2. I have no problem with the basics: grammar, spelling, and punctuation.			
3. I know the difference between active and passive constructions.			
4. I try to choose simple words to communicate clearly.			
5. I make it a point to state clearly the specific purpose of my letters or memos.			
6. I recognize and avoid business clichés and jargon.			
7. I ruthlessly edit everything I write.			
8. I'm confident I can communicate persuasively.			

Activity

Pair up and talk about your strengths and weaknesses in writing.

Punctuation Pointers

With spelling, people usually fall into one of two categories-good spellers or poor spellers. Punctuation errors, on the other hand, can trouble everyone.

COMMA (,)
SEMICOLON (;)
COLON (:)
APOSTROPHE (')

Fortunately, of the 30 main punctuation marks, business writing requires fewer than a dozen. Of these, the comma, semicolon, colon, and apostrophe are used most often and often incorrectly!

COMMA (,)

The comma sets off or separates words or groups of words within sentences.

Six Rules for the Comma

1. Use a comma after a long introductory phrase.
   After working all day at the office, I went home for dinner.
2. If the introductory phrase is short, forget the comma.
   After work I went home for dinner.
3. Use the comma if the sentence would be confusing without it.
   The day before, I borrowed her calculator.
   When you've finished, your dinner is ready.
4. Use the comma to separate items in a series.
   I need to pack my computer, calculator, business cards, and toothbrush.
5. Use a comma to separate two sentences that are joined by **and, but, or, nor, for, so, yet.**
   She liked her new job, and she respected her colleagues.
   He wanted the promotion, but he was afraid to ask his boss.
   They may go to the game, or they may stay here.
   The partners aren't going to the retreat, nor are they happy about it.
   Her assistant took a cab, for it was a long way to work.
   They waited until Friday, so it was too late to go.
   I'd like to travel, yet I'm reluctant to change jobs.
6. Use a comma to set off nonessential elements in a sentence.
   At the podium stood a man wearing a green tie.
   At the podium stood Frank, wearing a green tie.

In the first sentence, "wearing a green tie" is used to identify a specific man. Without it, the reader wouldn't know whom the writer was referring to, so it's essential to the meaning of the sentence.

In the second sentence, the writer assumes the reader knows Frank. "Wearing a green tie" adds only descriptive information about Frank, but it's not essential to the meaning of the sentence.

Exercise 1-1 Pair up and discuss the difference in meaning of the following two sentences.

a. The computer that is in the hallway is brand new.
b. The computer, which is in the hallway, is brand new.

Exercise 1-2 Correct the green sentence below in any of the following ways.

A Comma No-No

In general, don't separate two sentences with a comma.

He bought his first car last fall, it never ran well.

1. Use a period in place of the comma

____

2. Use a comma plus a conjunction (and, but, or, nor, so, for, yet)

____

3. Use a semicolon

____

SEMICOLON (;)

The semicolon separates two independent clauses, but it keeps those two thoughts more tightly linked than a period can: "I type letters; he types bills." Use a semicolon before and a comma after the following words if the words come between two independent clauses.

accordingly hence moreover similarly also however
namely still besides likewise nevertheless then
consequently indeed nonetheless therefore furthermore
instead otherwise thus

Exercise 2 Put commas and semicolons appropriately in the following sentences.

a. I thought I had completed the project consequently I was surprised to hear about the additional work.
b. We have prepared your estimate however you should sign it by Friday.
c. The partners' retreat will be held in March therefore all business matters will be discussed then.

COLON (:)

A colon is a tip-off to get ready for what's next: a list, a long quotation, or an explanation. A colon separates independent clauses when the second clause explains or amplifies the first.

Fred was proud of his sister: she had been promoted to managing partner.

My new office contains the following items: a desk, a leather chair, and oak paneling.

There are two things to remember in a job interview: always arrive promptly and always dress appropriately.

APOSTROPHE (')

An apostrophe is used to form the possessive of nouns and some pronouns, such as indefinite pronouns (someone, somebody, anyone, anybody, etc.), and to mark the omission of letter(s) in a contraction.

If the noun is singular, add 's.

I enjoyed Betty's presentation.

Someone's coat is in the lobby.

The same applies for singular nouns ending in "s" like James.

This is James's new office.

If the singular noun ends in "s" (like "Jones"), add "es" and an apostrophe to make it both plural and possessive.

Here is the Joneses' tax information.

If the noun is plural, add an apostrophe after the "s."

Those are the clients' files.

If the noun is an irregular plural, add 's.

This is the women's lounge area.

Exercise 3

Punctuate the following sentences.
Then pair up and compare your answers with each other.

1. The executive watched the competition but the competition went ahead with the takeover.
2. During our meeting she was gracious but shrewd.
3. Today more women are becoming executives in corporations.
4. The job was difficult therefore he quit.
5. My suitcase contained files pencils books and paper.
6. We thought we would have to work late therefore we were happy to be home before dark.
7. My boss car was in the shop consequently she borrowed her husbands.
8. In preparation for the meeting Mr. Jones asked us to do three things set up the equipment dust the tables and empty the ashtrays.
9. We wanted to go to the partners meeting but we were unable to leave before the weekend.
10. Lois résumé arrived yesterday moreover she phoned for an interview next week.

Exercise 4 Correct any incorrect punctuation and spelling in the following letter.

Southwestern Corporation
333 LaSalle Street,
Chicago, IL 60610

March 29, 20xx

Mr. John C. Freemont
2929 East Sycamore Street
Chicago, IL 60601

Dear Mr. Freemont

Thank you for meeting with us, and for your time and effort in preparing for the intervue. We appreciate your occomodating us with a fllexable schedule.

We are in the final stages of processing your application and we need three more items for our files. Your social security number permanent home address and your date of birth; as soon as we get this information we can procede to complete your permanent records.

Everyone here at Southwestern Corporation is looking forward to working with you. And we are eager to have you begin as soon as possible. Please, call me as soon as you can with this information.

Sincerely,

Janet L. Estes
Senor Vice President

Exercise 5 Find the 10 mistakes and correct them.

Below is the first draft of an e-mail message about a business trip to the U.S. There are two mistakes in each of the following categories:

- spelling
- punctuation
- capitalization
- verb tenses
- prepositions

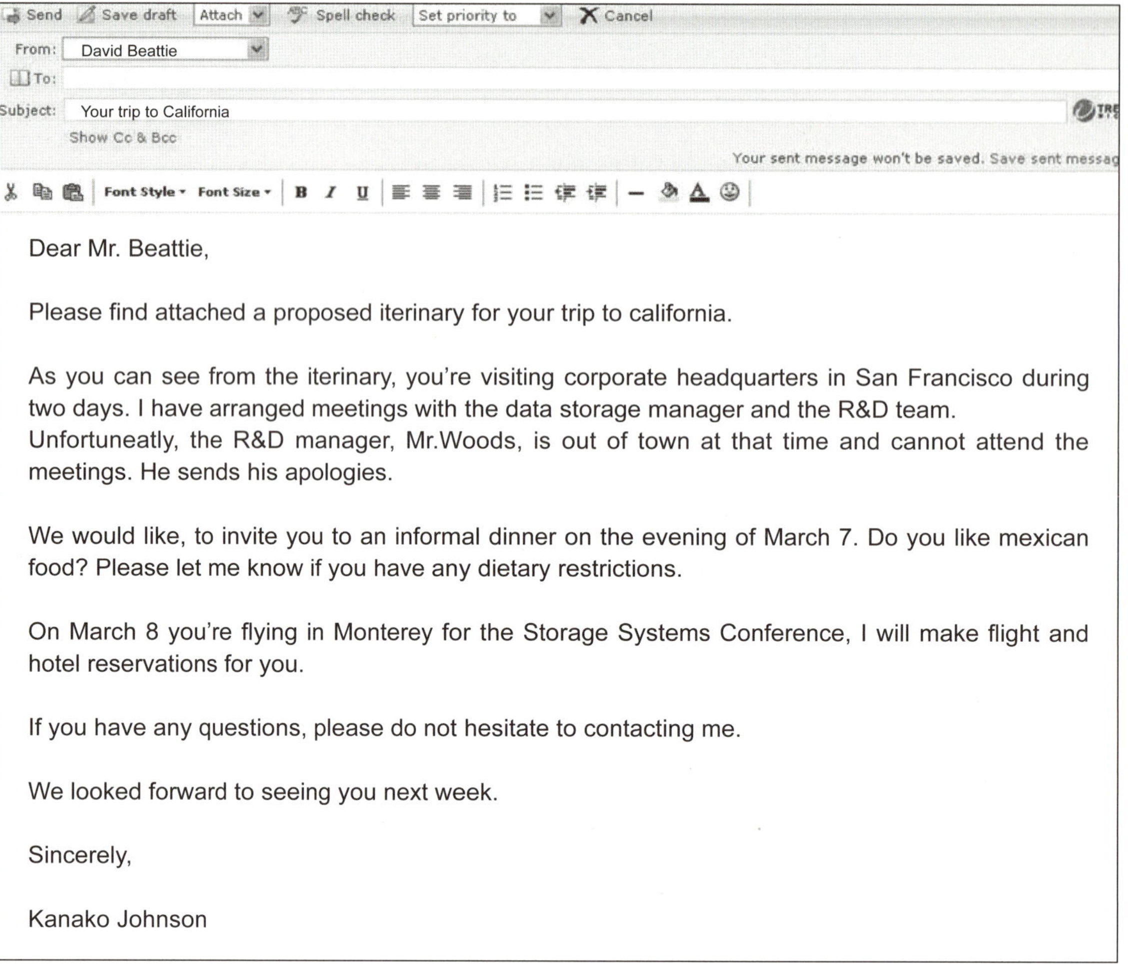

Send | Save draft | Attach | Spell check | Set priority to | Cancel

From: David Beattie

To:

Subject: Your trip to California

Show Cc & Bcc

Your sent message won't be saved. Save sent messag

Dear Mr. Beattie,

Please find attached a proposed iterinary for your trip to california.

As you can see from the iterinary, you're visiting corporate headquarters in San Francisco during two days. I have arranged meetings with the data storage manager and the R&D team. Unfortuneatly, the R&D manager, Mr.Woods, is out of town at that time and cannot attend the meetings. He sends his apologies.

We would like, to invite you to an informal dinner on the evening of March 7. Do you like mexican food? Please let me know if you have any dietary restrictions.

On March 8 you're flying in Monterey for the Storage Systems Conference, I will make flight and hotel reservations for you.

If you have any questions, please do not hesitate to contacting me.

We looked forward to seeing you next week.

Sincerely,

Kanako Johnson

Business Writing Simulation

Exercise 1-1 Read the e-mail quickly. Why is John writing?

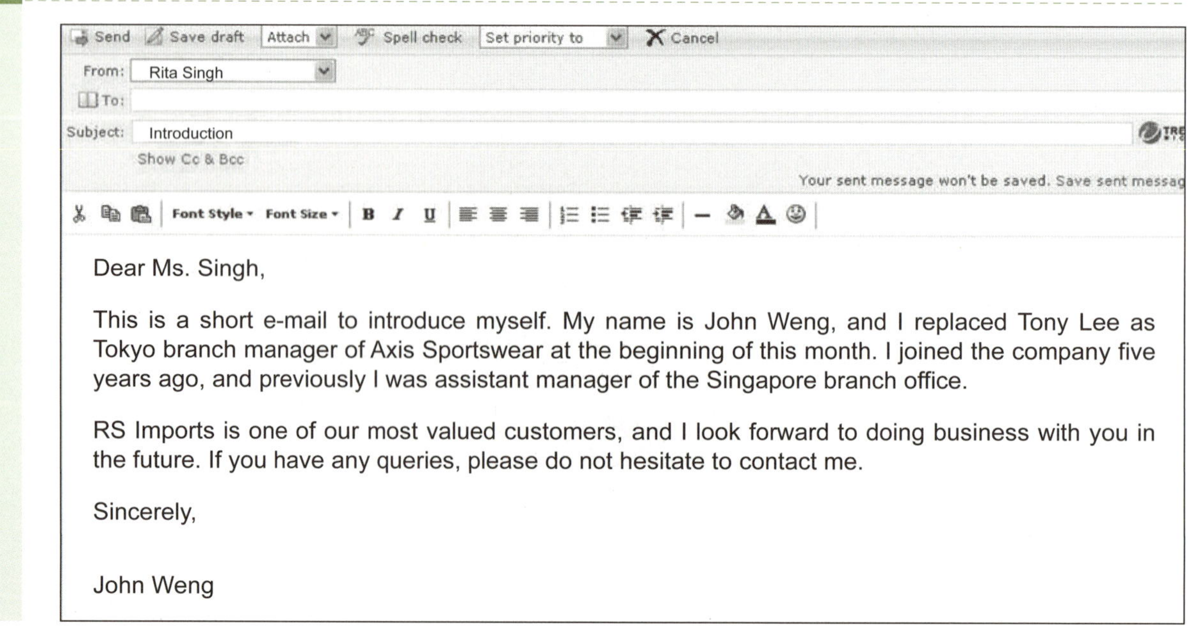

Send | Save draft | Attach | Spell check | Set priority to | Cancel

From: Rita Singh

To:

Subject: Introduction

Show Cc & Bcc

Your sent message won't be saved. Save sent messag

Dear Ms. Singh,

This is a short e-mail to introduce myself. My name is John Weng, and I replaced Tony Lee as Tokyo branch manager of Axis Sportswear at the beginning of this month. I joined the company five years ago, and previously I was assistant manager of the Singapore branch office.

RS Imports is one of our most valued customers, and I look forward to doing business with you in the future. If you have any queries, please do not hesitate to contact me.

Sincerely,

John Weng

Exercise 1-2

Are these statements true (T) or false (F)? Check (√)the correct box.

	T	F
a. John is writing to an old friend.	☐	☐
b. He started his new job last month.	☐	☐
c. He started working for Axis five years ago.	☐	☐
d. Rita Singh works for RS Imports.	☐	☐
e. John wants to meet with Ms. Singh very soon.	☐	☐

Exercise 1-3

Write the words and phrases in the e-mail that have the same or similar meanings as the ones below.

a. brief ____________________

b. started working for ____________________

c. before that ____________________

d. clients ____________________

e. working with ____________________

f. questions ____________________

g. feel free to ____________________

h. get in touch with ____________________

Exercise 1-4

Use the information below and the words and phrases in Exercise 1-3 to complete the introductory e-mail from Jenny Ho.

name: Jenny Ho
she replaced: Jim Baker
position: Marketing Manager
company: Viva Cosmetics
started new job: September 1
joined company: three years ago
previous position: sales representative

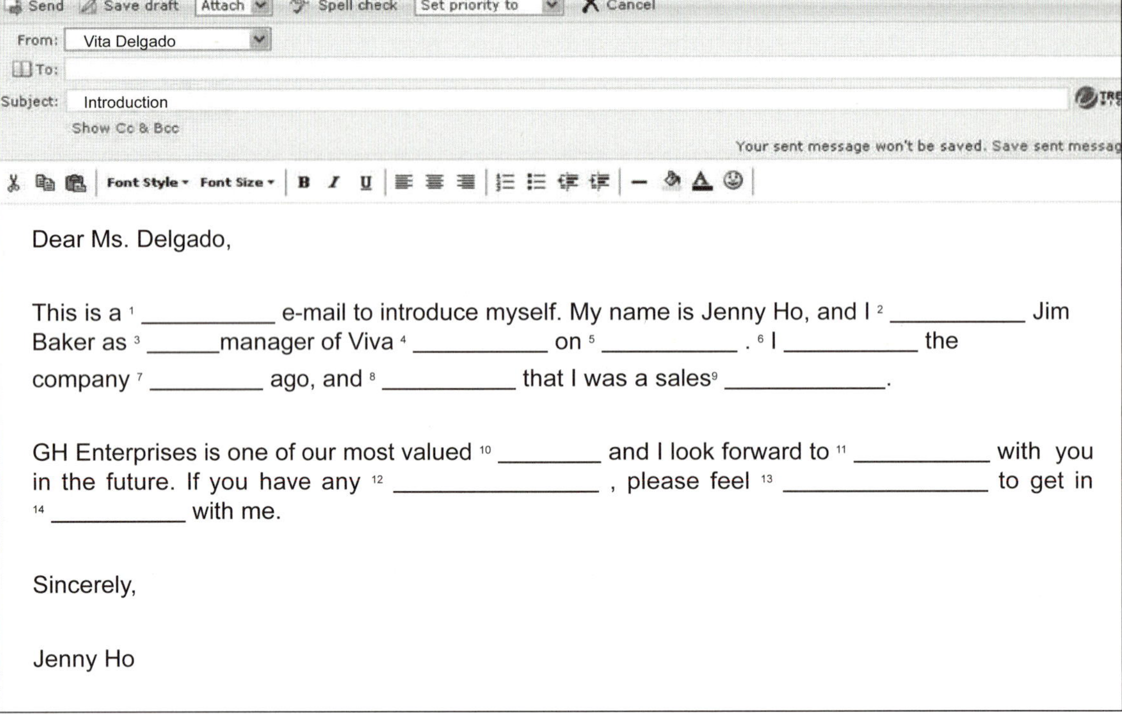

Dear Ms. Delgado,

This is a [1] __________ e-mail to introduce myself. My name is Jenny Ho, and I [2] __________ Jim Baker as [3] ______manager of Viva [4] __________ on [5] __________ . [6] I __________ the company [7] _________ ago, and [8] __________ that I was a sales[9] ____________.

GH Enterprises is one of our most valued [10] ________ and I look forward to [11] __________ with you in the future. If you have any [12] ______________ , please feel [13] ______________ to get in [14] __________ with me.

Sincerely,

Jenny Ho

Unit 2 Common Mistakes in Business Writing

Learning Objective:
After studying this unit, you should be able to....

- Understand the common mistakes in business writing.
- Write a business letter that will give your work clarity.

Questionnaire : Common mistakes in business writing

Following is a list of common problems in business writing.
What are the common mistakes you make in business writing?

Mistakes	*Check*	*Mistakes*	*Check*
1. Too many words		7. Sexist language	
2. Clichés		8. Negative expressions	
3. Too many big words		9. Inattention to detail	
4. Jargon		10. Inattention to the reader	
5. Vague expressions		11. Lack of commitment	
6. Condescending statements		12. Passive constructions	

Activity

Pair up and talk about what you checked in the above list, giving detailed examples. Then discuss possible solutions to your problems.

Pitfalls of Business Writing

Too many words

* One word is better than two.
* A good rule is to limit your sentences to fewer than 17 words.
* Edit ruthlessly.

Example

NOT: In this letter, we have attempted to answer all of your questions, and we hope that if you have any additional questions whatsoever, you will not hesitate to contact us.

BUT: If you have additional questions, please call us.

Clichés

* Avoid fad words and phrases like "input," "parameters," "utilize," "hopefully," and "enclosed please find."

Example

NOT: Enclosed please find the information per your request. Hopefully, you can utilize our product to benefit your company within the parameters of your computer's invoice processing. We appreciate your input.

BUT: We have enclosed the information you requested. Our product will speed your computer's invoice processing. Thank you for your suggestions.

Too many big words

* Keep your writing simple: use "home" instead of "abode," "face" instead of "visage," "use" instead of "utilize."
* Short words are better than long words.
* Try to be natural in your writing.
* Read your letters aloud after you write them; they should sound human and conversational.

Example

NOT: Pursuant to our discussion, herewith we acknowledge receipt of your correspondence as of the above date.

BUT: We received your letter on December 16 as we discussed.

NOT: The plumber discovered an excessive moisture condition in the bathroom pipes.

BUT: The plumber discovered a leak in the bathroom pipes.

Jargon

* Avoid unexplained terms like "facilitator" and "interface."
  What is a "modified departmentalized schedule?"

Example

NOT: Our facilitator will interface with the new communication systems network.

BUT: Our administrative assistant will operate the new telephone system.

Vague Expressions

* Be concise and specific.
  If the "profits were affected," did they increase or decrease?

Example

NOT: The company's negative cash flow position forced it to resize its operations to the level of profitable market opportunities.

BUT: The company lost money and had to lay off workers.

Condescending Statements

* Write with warmth, as one human to another.
  "Of course" can be interpreted to mean "As any idiot knows."

Example

NOT: We are certain you are concerned with saving money. Of course, you will mail the enclosed card. We thank you in advance.

BUT: If saving money is important to you, please mail the enclosed card today. Thank you.

Sexist language

* Consider your reader (the salutation "Gentlemen" is outdated).
* Traditionally, "he," "his," and "him" are considered acceptable to use as gender neutral pronouns, yet there are alternatives you can use to avoid offending your readers.
* Use "he or she" sparingly.

Example

NOT: An accountant must pass a difficult exam before he can become a CPA.

BUT: (use plurals) Accountants must pass a difficult exam before they can become CPAs.

Negative expressions

* Stress the positive.
* Instead of telling what you can't do or don't have, provide good news.

Example

NOT: We're sorry to tell you that we don't carry XYZ software.

BUT: Since we no longer carry XYZ software, we are sending you a list of distributors who do carry the software.

Inattention to detail

* Triple-check accuracy and quality.
* Reread for typos and misspelled words.

Example

NOT: We hope we can accomodate your office supply and stationaries needs.
BUT: We hope we can accommodate your office supply and stationary needs.

Inattention to the reader

* Write in the first person when appropriate.
* Write in the second person when possible.
* Remember to write with the readers' perspective in mind.

Example

NOT: We would like to invite you to attend the conference.
BUT: You are invited to attend the conference.

Lack of commitment

* Take a stand.
* Omit qualifiers-"sort of," "rather," "quite," "somewhat," etc.

Example

NOT: We are quite pleased about our rather exciting word processor.
BUT: We are pleased about our exciting line of word processors.

Passive Construction

* Use active verbs.
* The normal order of sentences is subject (performer of action), verb, and object (receiver of action). In passive construction, the order is reversed: the object is first, followed by a form of the verb "be" (am, is, are, was, were, been, being) before the main verb in the past participle form. The subject is last (usually preceded by the word "by").

Example

NOT: The check was signed by my boss. [7 words]
The letter is being typed by the secretary. [8 words]
BUT: My boss signed the check. [5 words]
The secretary is typing the letter. [6 words]

Exercise 1 Revise the following sentences by yourself. Then pair up and compare your answers.

1. (Too many words) This note is to let you know that we are sponsoring a company picnic next month in Lincoln Grove. If you need directions, please don't hesitate to contact us.
   →

2. (Clichés) Please be advised that at the present time we have no available job openings. Thank you for your interest.
   →

3. (Too many big words) Prior to departure, please terminate the illumination.
   →

4. (Passive construction) Our request for an increase in salary will be considered by the board at its next meeting.
   →

Parallel Construction

Parallel construction adds clarity, elegance, and symmetry to your writing. Words, phrases, and statements are coordinated to be grammatically parallel: noun aligned with noun, verb with verb, and phrase with phrase. For example:

1. NOT : Speaking in public is sometimes harder than to write in private.
   BUT : Speaking in public is sometimes harder than writing in private.
2. NOT : My partner is a man of action, decision, and who is bright.
   BUT : My partner is a man of action, decision, and intelligence.
3. NOT : Sarah's office was painted, had carpeting put in, and paneled last week.
   BUT : Sarah's office was painted, carpeted, and paneled last week.
4. NOT : To teach, to supervise, and delegating work are a few of the tasks our office manager performs.
   BUT : Teaching, supervising, and delegating work are a few of the tasks our office manager performs.

Parallel construction not only adds symmetry, but also often reduces wordiness-see examples 2 and 3 above. Don't hesitate, however, to repeat a word if it makes your sentence clearer. For example:

1. NOT : She has and continues to seem competent.
   BUT : She has seemed and continues to seem competent.
2. NOT : A secretary can program a computer to type a letter but not think.
   BUT : A secretary can program a computer to type a letter but not to think.

When you proofread your work, check for parallel construction. The additional clarity and economy will add polish to your style.

Exercise 2 Revise the following sentences using correct parallel construction. If the sentence is already parallel, write "No change."

1. It was both a long meeting and very tedious.
2. Joe likes a job with challenging work that keeps him stimulated.
3. Poor writing wastes time, costs money, and customers feel alienated.
4. Presentations should be concise, stimulating, and interactive.
5. Overseas clients are impressed with our company's hospitality and thoughtfulness.

Business Writing Simulation

Exercise 1-1 Read the e-mails quickly and answer the questions.

a. Why is Mr. Roussos writing?

b. Can Ms. Kapoor meet him on Friday?

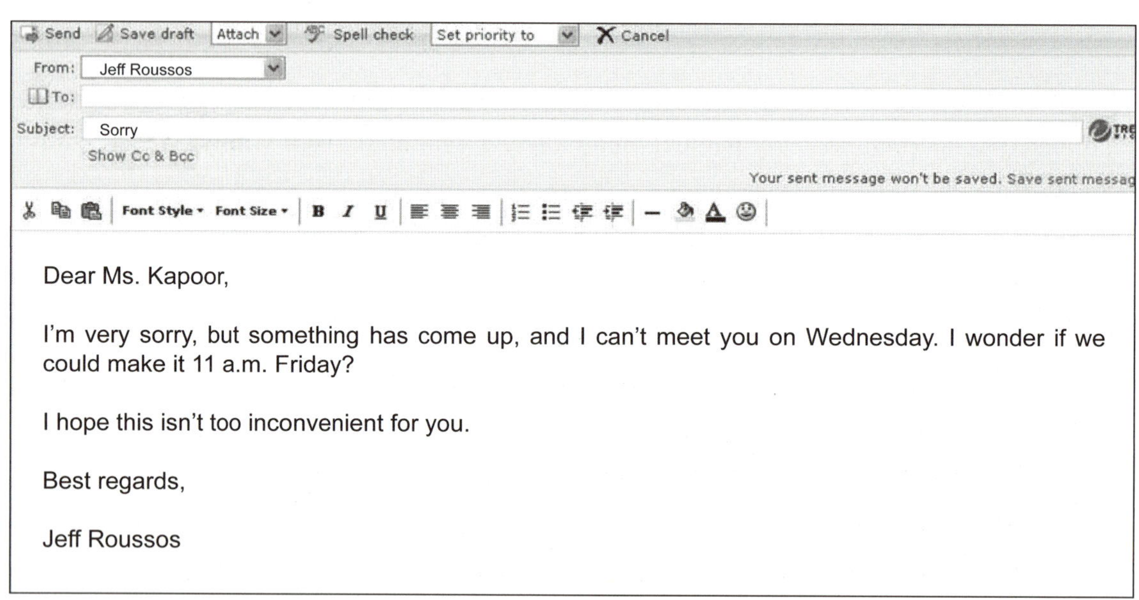

Send Save draft Attach Spell check Set priority to Cancel

From: Jeff Roussos

To:

Subject: Sorry

Show Cc & Bcc

Your sent message won't be saved. Save sent messag

Font Style Font Size

Dear Ms. Kapoor,

I'm very sorry, but something has come up, and I can't meet you on Wednesday. I wonder if we could make it 11 a.m. Friday?

I hope this isn't too inconvenient for you.

Best regards,

Jeff Roussos

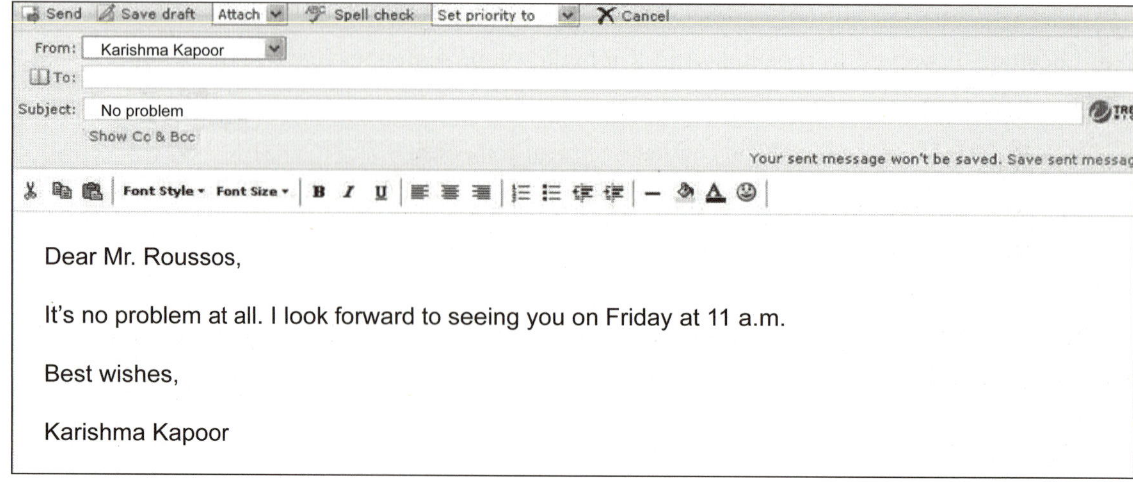

Send Save draft Attach Spell check Set priority to Cancel

From: Karishma Kapoor

To:

Subject: No problem

Show Cc & Bcc

Your sent message won't be saved. Save sent messag

Font Style Font Size

Dear Mr. Roussos,

It's no problem at all. I look forward to seeing you on Friday at 11 a.m.

Best wishes,

Karishma Kapoor

Exercise 1-2 LANGUAGE FOCUS

If you cannot keep an appointment, you can start:			
I'm (very) sorry, but I'm afraid	I had something urgent come up for next week, / I have to change my plans for next week,	and	I won't be able to meet with you on Thursday. / it's not possible for me to meet you on Thursday.
Suggest another time and / or place: I wonder if we could reschedule it for 11 a.m. Friday? Would 11 a.m. Friday be possible?			
End with an apology: I'm sorry for the trouble. I'm very sorry about the inconvenience.			
When you respond to a change in plans, you can use:			
It's no	trouble inconvenience	at all.	Friday at 11 a.m. will be no problem. 11 a.m. Friday is fine with me.

Rewrite the e-mails in Exercise 1-1 using the alternative phrases above.
Use the same days and times.

A ______________________________

____

____

____

B ______________________________

____

____

____

Unit 3 Format of Business Letters

Learning Objective:

After studying this unit, you should be able to....

- Understand the different kinds of business letter formats.
- Write a business letter that looks professional and will make an impact.

Questionnaire : What are the parts of a business letter?

Business letters are an indispensable part of business communication. Without them, much of the ordinary activities of business would not be possible.

Most business letters, regardless of their purpose, have the following basic parts. Check the parts you usually include in your business letters.

Parts of a business letter	*Check*
1. Heading or letterhead	
2. Date	
3. Inside address	
4. Reference lines (attention, personal and confidential, subject)	
5. Salutation	
6. Body	
7. Complimentary closing	
8. Signature	
9. Stenographic reference	
10. Enclosures or copies	

Activity

Among the parts of a business letter above, are there any parts you don't clearly understand? Pair up and talk about each part of a business letter.

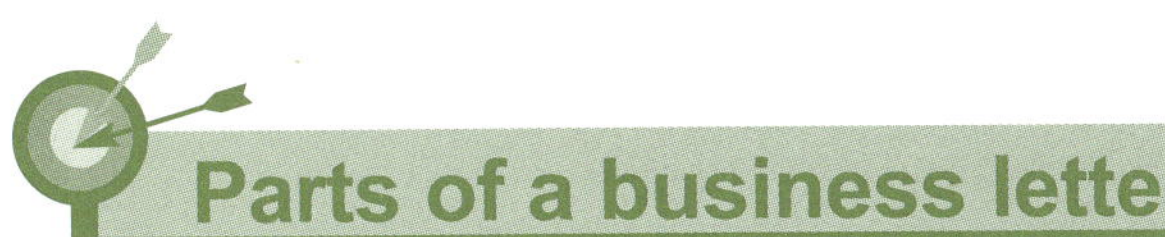

Parts of a business letter

Heading or letterhead

In most cases, the heading of a letter is simply the printed letterhead giving the company name, address(es), phone number(s), and perhaps the name of an officer or correspondent. If there is no printed letterhead, type the company information in the upper right-hand corner of the paper.

[Example of a letterhead]

Date

The date records when the letter was written and may serve as an important reference.

Example

August 16, 2007

Inside address

The inside address contains the name, title, company division or department, company name, mailing address, and zip code of the receiver.

Example

Mr. Alfred McKenna, Treasurer
Finance and Accounting Department
Warren, Hanson & Associates
459 Third Avenue
New York, New York 10017

Reference lines

When you want to call special attention to the subject of the letter or single out a particular person to whom the letter is addressed in a company, you can use a reference.

"Personal and Confidential" comes before the inside address, while "Attention" and "Subject" are typed below the inside address with a colon following.

Example

Personal and Confidential
Ms. Jane Purdy, Vice President
Trust Department
First National Bank of Atlanta
900 Grove Street
Atlanta, Georgia 30319

Mr. Earl Jacobs, Sales Manager
Merchant's Restaurant
633 South Dearborn
Leland, Kansas 67073

Subject: Delivery of red snapper catch

Salutation

The salutation is typed two lines down, flush with the left margin, and followed by a colon.

Example

Dear Ms. (or Miss or Mrs.) Culver:
Dear Mr. Jacobs:

If you do not know the name of the recipient but do know that you will be addressing a man or woman, your salutation would be as the following examples.

Example

Dear Sir:
Dear Madam:

If you do not know whom the receiver will be, use a title or some general greeting for salutation.

Example

Dear Friends at Royal:
Dear Manager:
Dear Executive:
Dear Members:
To the Sales Staff:

Body of the letter

The body can be typed in block style with no paragraph indentations or semiblock style in which the paragraphs are indented. There is no "correct" style.

It is best, even for a short letter, to divide the body into at least two or three paragraphs. This step makes your text easier to read and presents your message more clearly.

Complimentary closing

The complimentary closing can be centered on the page or set flush with the left or right margin. The preferred complimentary closing for most business letters is "Sincerely," although many companies also use "Yours truly" or "Sincerely yours."

The closing is followed by four lines and the typed name and title of the person sending the letter.

Example

Sincerely,

Frank W. Weston
Vice President, Distribution
(878)999-6200

Signature

The writer signs his or her name in ink in the space between the complementary closing and the typed name.

Stenographic reference

These reference initials refer to the person who is sending the letter and to the typist. The sender's initials are typed in all capitals, followed by a colon or a slash, then the initials of the typist in lowercase letters.

Example

FWW:tg or FWW/tg

Enclosures or copies

This designation is typed one single space below the stenographic initials. It alerts the reader to the fact that material has been enclosed with the letter or that copies of the letter have been sent to others.

Example

Encl: or Enclosures: (5) or Enclosures: Map
Brochure
Car rentals
Hotel list

Cc: or Copies: R. Hanlin, Treasurer
M. McKenna, Secretary
T. Freund, Sales Manager

Exercise 1 Pair up and answer the following questions.

1. The part that delivers the message: __Body__
2. The part that includes the reader's name and address: ________________
3. The part that includes the writer's company name, address, phone, and fax numbers: ________________
4. The part that should be signed, not printed: ________________
5. The part that indicates something is being sent with the letter: ________________

Exercise 2-1 Read the letter.

October 6, 2004

EBA Business
475 Western Avenue
Melbourn 3001
Victoria
Australia

Dear Sir/Madam:

I am hoping to visit Australia later this year, and I recently saw your advertisement about the EBA business program in "Business World" magazine.

Could you please send me a copy of your latest catalog?

I look forward to hearing from you.

Sincerely,

Maria Rivera

Maria Rivera

Exercise 2-2 Answer the questions.

a. Which company is Maria writing to?
b. Why doesn't she write a person's name in the salutation?
c. In which magazine did she see the advertisement?
d. What does she ask the company to do?

Exercise 2-3

Look at these parts of a letter to RBM Manufacturing company, Inc. Write them in the correct position in the letter.

May 2, 2005

RBM Manufacturing Company, Inc.

11295 9th Avenue

New York, New York 10055

We would also like to know about your warranty and repair service.

William Wilson

William Wilson

Office Manager at MM Industries

Since our fiscal year ends June 30, 2005, we hope to hear from you soon.

We intend to purchase a new laser printer/copier before the end of the fiscal year. We would like to consider an RBM copier.

We run approximately 3000 copies a month and prefer a machine with fax capability. We would like a collator, but rarely need to run off more than 25 copies at any one time.

Dear Sir or Madam:

Sincerely yours,

____

____

____

____

____

____

____

____

____

____

____

____

____

____

____

____

Business Writing Simulation

Question

You work at Crescent Finance Company, 71-75 Langan Road, Dublin 11, Ireland (telephone 870 3269). Mrs. Colette Doherty, the owner of the firm, hands you the following letter which she has received and asks you to draft a letter in reply ready for her signature. She says, "I remember Sunil very well. I was sorry that he left us. He was a good worker and he got on well with his colleagues."

Shamrock Bank

Springfield Road Bishopstown Cork (telephone 021 271863)

(date)
Mrs. Colette Doherty
Crescent Finance Company
71-75 Langan Road
Dublin 11

RE: Mr. Sunil Cheema (date of birth March 15, 1970)

Dear Mrs. Doherty:
Mr. Cheema has applied for a job in our Accounts Department.

He has given your name as a reference and states that he worked for your firm for 3 years in the Sales Support Department before leaving in order to gain higher qualifications at Cork University.

I shall be grateful for any comments which may help us in considering his application.

I thank you for your cooperation.

Yours sincerely,

Maeve Nolan

Maeve Nolan
Manager

You check in the personnel files and find the following information:

Surname CHEEMA	Forename Sunil
Date of birth	March 15, 1970
Date of appointment	September 6, 1994
Date of leaving	August 12, 1997
Reason for leaving	to attend Cork University to follow a 3-year course leading to the degree of Bachelor of Science in Information Technology and Accounts
Career at Crescent Finance	September 1994 - December 1994 Introductory Course (Sales) January 1995 - August 1997 Sales Support Team offered promotion August 1997
Training	short courses in: • Computers • Customer Service •Accounting
Comments	pleasant personality, intelligent never late absent from work 10 days (illness)

Write the letter.

Unit 4 Revision in Business Writing

Learning Objective:

After studying this unit, you should be able to....

- Write a rough draft clearly and effectively.
- Write a business letter to insure that you've said exactly what you meant to say in a manner that the reader will understand.

Questionnaire : Why edit?

We edit for a few reasons. It saves time by allowing you to write more freely, allows more thorough review with more objectivity, and produces a better finished product. Before you begin, answer the following questions.

	Yes	No	I don't know
1. Do I accomplish my objective when writing?			
2. Do I cover the subject sufficiently?			
3. Is my writing logical and thorough?			
4. Do I anticipate my reader's objections and address them?			
5. Do I explain any unclear terms or references?			
6. Is my letter easy to read and understand?			

Activity

Pair up and talk about how you can effectively revise a business letter based on the answers you gave above.

Revision requires a shift in your perspective

To revise effectively, you must first distance yourself from your writing so that you can respond objectively. In other words, you need to shift your perspective by assuming the role of the reader. To accomplish this, you should get away from the paper for a while, usually leaving it until the following morning. You may not be able to budget your time this ideally; but you can put the paper aside while you visit a friend, grab a bite to eat, or work on something else. Unless you divorce yourself from the paper, you will probably remain under its spell: that is, you will see only what you think is on the page instead of what is actually there. And you will be unable to transport yourself from your role of writer to that of reader.

Such objective distance may at first seem difficult to achieve; however, the following suggestions should help you to systematize the revision stage of your letter and report writing and enable you to keep your reader in mind as you determine appropriate language.

Language: Aiming for conciseness and clarity

1. You should use only the essential words to get your message across to your reader.

Example

It is the responsibility of our Production Department to see that it meets the requirements of our Sales Division. (19 words)

→ Our Production Department must meet our Sales Division's requirements. (9 words)

Exercise 1 Change the following wordy sentences to concise sentences. Then pair up and exchange your answers.

a. The sale of surplus products is one of our primary goals.

b. This manual of instructions was prepared to aid our dealers in being helpful to their customers.

c. The collision had the effect of a destructive force on the duplicator.

d. We have enclosed a pamphlet which shows further details of the construction on page four.

2. You should try not to use too many words when you express simple, unimportant, or obvious ideas.

Example

Three days ago you asked us to investigate the problem of discomfort among your office workers... We have made our study. The low level of humidity is apparently the main cause of your problem. Your building is steam-heated; therefore, your solution is to... (43 words)

→ The low level of humidity is apparently the cause of your workers' discomfort. Since your building is steam-heated, your solution is to... (22 words)

3. You should not pour out ideas and facts too rapidly for the reader's comprehension.

Negative example

Our deluxe models have chromium, rubber-insulated fixtures for durability, economy, and easy maintenance, and convenient controls to cut down on installation costs and necessary adjustments. They operate on AC or DC current and incorporate the latest principles of electronic controls which means flexibility in their use, better adjustment of the thermal units, less chance of error, and reduced labor costs per unit of production.

4. You should use more vivid and convincing specific words instead of vague words.

Example

contact → call, write, visit

slowly → about as fast as you normally walk

soon → by March 15

This television set is high quality. → All components in this television set meet or exceed government specifications for use in manned satellites.

5. You should use more direct and accessible words rather than excessive or overwritten words.

Example

The defendant is renowned as a person of intemperate habits. He is known to partake heavily of intoxicating beverages. Further, he cultivates the company of others of the distaff side, and wholly, regularly, and consistently refuses and abstains from earnest endeavors to gain remuneration.

→ The defendant drinks, chases after women, and refuses to work.

Exercise 2-1

Read the six extracts from correspondence to colleagues and business acquaintances and write the correct letter (a-f) next to each one.

a. a letter thanking a speaker for a presentation to a business association
b. an e-mail congratulating a colleague on her promotion
c. a letter to a colleague expressing sympathy about an accident
d. an e-mail to a colleague who is retiring
e. a message on a condolence card to the wife of a business acquaintance
f. a message on a seasonal greeting card to a business acquaintance

1 ☐

We hope you'll make a speedy recovery and hope to see you soon.

2 ☐

We were shocked to hear of Tetsuo's sudden death. We had the greatest respect for him and know that he will be greatly missed by everyone.

3 ☐

I am sure that you will be a great success in your new position. Let's stay in touch.

4 ☐

Martina and I hope you are all well. We send our good wishes for the new year!

5 ☐

Everyone found the evening enjoyable and inspiring, and we hope that you will be able to address our group again next year.

6 ☐

I am sure you are looking forward to having more time to play golf. I know that we are all going to miss you.

Exercise 2-2

Write the words and phrases in the extracts above which have the same or similar meanings to the items below:

a. quick ______________

b. unexpected ______________

c. job ______________

d. in good health ______________

e. speak to ______________

f. certain ______________

Exercise 3

LANGUAGE FOCUS

<table>
<tr><td colspan="4">You can use this language to congratulate someone formally:</td></tr>
<tr><td colspan="2">Please accept my congratulations</td><td rowspan="2">on</td><td rowspan="2">your promotion.
receiving this year's sales award.</td></tr>
<tr><td>I would like to
I'm writing to</td><td>congratulate you</td></tr>
<tr><td colspan="4">Use these phrases for more informal congratulations:</td></tr>
<tr><td colspan="2">Congratulations on</td><td colspan="2">your graduation!
the new arrival!</td></tr>
</table>

Write sentences for the situations below. Use a different expression each time.
Congratulate:

a. a co-worker on her promotion (informal)

____

____

b. a business acquaintance on the opening of his company's Milan branch (formal)

____

____

c. a co-worker on his twentieth year of employment with your company (formal)

____

____

Exercise 4

Circle the correct word in each pair, and then write the corrected letter.

Dear Vernon,

I am [1] **writing / write** to congratulate you [2] **on / to** your appointment [3] **as / for** Vice President of GL Electronics.

I know that you [4] **will / have** achieve great success in your new job, and I look forward to continued [5] **co-operate / co-operation** between our two [6] **company / companies.**

Sincerely yours,

Miranda Finkelstein

Miranda Finkelstein

____

____

____

____

____

____

____

Exercise 5

LANGUAGE FOCUS

To express sympathy for an illness or accident, you can use:				
I was very We were so	sorry to hear of	your	illness. accident.	
For condolences, you can use:				
I was We were	(deeply)	shocked/saddened	to hear of	your husband's death. Matthew's passing.

Use the expressions to complete the letter of sympathy to Mei (A) and letter of condolence to Sergei (B).

a. Just concentrate on getting better.
b. if there is anything I can do to help.
c. my sincerest sympathy at this difficult time.
d. I hope you get well soon.

Dear Mei,

I was very sorry to hear about your accident, and ______________________________

____

____

____

Don't worry about work for a while

____

____

We all look forward to welcoming you back to the office when you are ready.

With very best wishes,

Tom Nakamura

Dear Sergei,

I was deeply saddened to hear of the death of your mother. Please accept

____

____

____

Please let me know

____

____

____

Sincerely,

Elaine Border

Business Writing Simulation

Following is a memo sent by the President of XYZ Company to all employees. Revise this memo to make it clearer, shorter, and friendlier.

MEMORANDUM

TO: All Employees

FROM: The President

DATE: September 15, 20xx

RE: Staff Meeting

XYZ Company wishes to inform all employees of the postponement of the previously scheduled staff meeting. This cancellation is due to a current pressing financial situation of this company.

This firm has faced a significant drop in the sales volume for the past six months. Our response to these pressing issues must be to make more productive use of our time and effect an increase in the sales volume.

This staff meeting will be postponed immediately until further notice by the president. Employees will be informed of further developments regarding rescheduling our meeting and our financial situation.

MEMORANDUM

TO: ______________________

FROM: ______________________

DATE: ______________________

RE: ______________________

Unit 5 Tone in Business Writing

Learning Objective:

After studying this unit, you should be able to....

- Learn to write and handle negative and argumentative tones with sensitivity and care.
- Adapt your business letter to the needs and level of your readers.

Questionnaire : Tailoring tone in business writing

When you are tailoring the tone of your business writing, what do you consider among the following questions?

Questions	*Check*
1. Have I expressed my ideas so that the reader will feel that I am helpful, courteous, and human?	
2. Have I tailored my message to my reader's desires, problems, circumstances, and probable reactions to the purpose of my message?	
3. Have I emphasized "you", the reader, instead of "I" or "we"?	
4. Have I expressed my ideas so they reflect good public relations for the company (letters) or good human relations with my colleagues (reports)?	
5. Have I tactfully avoided words and phrases which imply that my reader is dishonest, careless, or mentally deficient?	
6. Have I stressed the positive and avoided emphasizing ideas my reader may view unfavorably?	

Activity

Pair up and discuss what kind of things you consider the most or pass over among the questions above. Explain the reasons for your answers.

Setting the Right Tone

Business writers should consider the tone of their message, whether they are writing a memo, letter, report, or any type of business document. Tone is present in all communication activities. Ultimately, the tone of a message is a reflection of the writer and it does affect how the reader will perceive the message.

Fortunately, you can use the same kind of tone for most business messages. The business writer should strive for an overall tone that is confident, courteous, and sincere; that uses emphasis and subordination appropriately; that contains nondiscriminatory language; that stresses the "you" attitude; and that is written at an appropriate level of difficulty. The only major exceptions to these guidelines are when you need to write a negative business message, such as when you deny a job offer or a customer request.

Here are some general guidelines to keep in mind when considering what kind of tone to use in your letters and how to present information in that tone:

- Be confident.
- Be courteous and sincere.
- Use appropriate emphasis and subordination.
- Use non-discriminatory language.
- Stress the benefits for the reader.
- Write at an appropriate level of difficulty.

Be confident

You can feel confident if you have carefully prepared and are knowledgeable about the material you wish to express. The manner in which you write should assume a confident tone as well. As you prepare business documents, you want the reader to do as you ask or to accept your decision. In order to make the document effective, you must write confidently.

Consequently, a confident tone will have a persuasive effect on your audience. The reader will become more inclined to accept your position and will notice the confidence that you have. Employers are inclined to hire individuals that appear confident and sure of their abilities.

This does not mean, however, that you should appear overconfident. This can easily be interpreted as arrogant or presumptuous.

Example

You must agree that I am qualified for the position.

→ My qualifications in the areas of accounting and customer service meet your job requirements.

Be courteous and sincere

A writer builds goodwill for him or herself by using a tone that is polite and sincere. It is important to strive for sincerity in tone because without sincerity, politeness can sound condescending.

Consider the words and phrases you use in your document and how your reader will likely receive them. If you are respectful and honest, readers will be more willing to accept your message, even if it is negative.

Exercise 1 Pair up and try to change the sentence to make it sound more courteous and sincere.

You didn't read the instructions carefully, thus your system has shut down.

Use appropriate emphasis and subordination

You can help your readers to understand which of your ideas you consider most important by using emphasis and subordination. To emphasize an idea, place it in a short sentence. A short and simple sentence will most effectively convey an important idea. To subordinate an idea, place it in a compound sentence.

Example of emphasis

Smoking will no longer be permitted in the building. The Committee on Employee Health and Safety reached this decision after considering evidence from researchers and physicians on the dangers of second-hand smoke.

Example of subordination

The Committee on Employee Health and Safety has finished considering evidence, and they have reached the decision that smoking will no longer be permitted in the building.

Use nondiscriminatory language

Nondiscriminatory language is language that treats all people equally. It does not use any words, remarks, or ideas that reflect prejudice.

Examples of nondiscriminatory language

Suggestion	Not:	But:
Use neutral job titles.	Chairman	Chairperson
Avoid demeaning or stereotypical terms.	After the girls in the office receive an order, our office fills it within 24 hours.	When orders are received at our office, they are filled within 24 hours.
Avoid words and phrases that unnecessarily imply gender.	Executives and their wives	Executives and their spouses

Exercise 2 Pair up and try to change the sentences to avoid discriminatory language.

Suggestion	*Not:*	*But:*
Omit information about group membership.	Connie Green performed the job well for her age.	
If you do not know a reader's gender, use a nonsexist salutation.	Dear Gentlemen: Each student must provide	
Do not use masculine pronouns.	his own lab jacket.	

Stress the benefits for the reader

Instead of simply writing from the perspective of what the reader can do for you, write with the reader's perspective in mind in a way that shows what you can do for the reader. A reader will often read a document wondering "What's in it for me?" It is your job to tailor your document accordingly. Stressing reader benefits will help you to avoid sounding self-centered and uninterested.

Exercise 3 Pair up and try to change the sentence to benefit the reader.

I am processing your order tomorrow.
→

Write at an appropriate level of difficulty

It is essential that you write at an appropriate level of difficulty in order to clearly convey your message. Adjust your style of writing to match the reading abilities of your audience. A competent writer will match the needs and abilities of their reader and find the most effective way to communicate with a particular reader.

Writing negative messages

It is especially important to consider tone when you are writing a negative message. In a negative message, such as a document that rejects a job offer or denies a request, be sure to assume a tone that is gracious and sincere. Thank the reader for their input or involvement and carefully state that you cannot comply with their wishes. Follow this response with an explanation as necessary.

It is best not to draw attention to the person performing the action that will likely displease the reader. Therefore, you may want to avoid using active voice when delivering negative messages. You might also avoid stressing the reader benefits unless there are clear benefits to the negative message. It can sound insincere to stress reader benefits in a negative message.

In some negative messages, you may need to address faults or issues concerning an individual. When writing messages such as this, maintain a professional tone that does not attack the individual but that makes your position on the issue clear.

Example

I do not understand why you made such discriminatory remarks.
→ Discriminatory remarks are not tolerated in this organization.

Exercise 4 Change the negative tone of the following letter to a more positive one.

Thank you for offering me the position as General Manager at Simon's Inc. Unfortunately, I am unable to accept the position. I did not think that the position you offered me would utilize my communication and customer service skills to the degree that I wanted. Therefore, I have accepted a position as Assistant Director at a different company.

Business Writing Simulation

Read the following situation and write a letter accordingly. Keep in mind the following:

1. Be confident.
2. Be courteous and sincere.
3. Use appropriate emphasis and subordination.
4. Use non-discriminatory language.
5. Stress the benefits for the reader.
6. Write at an appropriate level of difficulty.

<Situation>

Suzy is writing a job acceptance letter to an employer but is unsure of the tone she should take in the message. She has decided to accept the position. When she asks herself, "What is my intent upon writing?" she answers, "I want to accept the position, thank the company for the offer, and establish goodwill with my new co-workers." As she writes the letter she quickly assumes a tone that is appreciative for the offer and enthusiastic about beginning a new job.

<Writing worksheet>

Unit 6 Inquiry and Request Letters

Learning Objective:
After studying this unit, you should be able to....

- Write inquiry letters with clarity.
- Write replies to request letters that both provide an answer and strengthen public relations.

Questionnaire : What are the proper steps for developing an inquiry letter?

Following are some items that you should include in your inquiry letters. Put the items in the correct order. The first one has been done for you.

What you should include	Order
List the specific information you need. You can phrase your requests as questions or as a list of specific items of information. In either case, make each item clear and discrete.	
Conclude your letter by offering your reader some incentive for responding.	
Identify yourself and, if appropriate, your position and your institution or firm.	1
Briefly explain why you are writing and how you will use the requested information. Offer to keep the response confidential if such an offer seems reasonable.	

Activity

Pair up and discuss what you should consider when you write an inquiry letter.

Inquiry Letters

A letter of inquiry asks someone for specific information. In some cases, such as a request for promotional material, the recipient will have a clear interest in responding to your letter. In other cases, such as a request for specific information on a product, the recipient may or may not be as motivated to respond quickly. Consequently, always make the tone of the letter friendly and make it easy for the recipient to identify and provide the information you need.

Key Tips on Inquiry:

- Whenever you seek a written response to an unsolicited inquiry, include a stamped, self-addressed envelope for the reply.
- While unsolicited inquires via telephone or e-mail can be efficient and productive, they can also be unwelcome and intrusive. A traditional letter implies greater respect for the recipient's privacy and provides a certain distance from which the person can choose to respond or even decide not to respond.
- If you choose to inquire via traditional letter you may also choose to give the recipient the option of responding via phone or e-mail. If you do go the route of telephone or e-mail, establish a brief contact in which you apologize for any intrusion. Next, ask about the respondent's willingness to answer your questions now or at a convenient time in the near future.
- In all cases of inquiry, don't let your time constraints or efficiency compromise your goodwill.
- Always write a thank-you note to the person who has responded to your inquiry letter.

Exercise 1-1

Read the e-mail to a machine manufacturer quickly. What does Etsuko want the company to send? Check(√) the correct box.

a. machinery ☐
b. information ☐
c. plastic household goods ☐

Send | Save draft | Attach | Spell check | Set priority to | Cancel

From: marketing@plas.com
To:
Subject: Catalog request
Show Cc & Bcc

Your sent message won't be saved. Save sent messa

Font Style · Font Size · B I U

Dear Wesplas:

We saw your advertisement in Plastics Monthly and would like to know more about your molding machines.

As you may know, Plascom is a successful manufacturer of high quality plastic household goods with an extensive sales network throughout East and Southeast Asia. We are planning to replace our molding machines in the near future.

Would you please send us your latest catalog, including a full price list and details of discounts? Please send them to the address below.

I look forward to hearing from you.

Sincerely,

Etsuko Goto
Assistant Production Controller
Plascom
1-30-6 Nishi Gotanda
Shinagawa-ku
Tokyo, Japan
142-8436

Exercise 1-2 Answer the questions.

a. Why doesn't Etsuko write a person's name in the salutation?
b. In which magazine did she see the advertisement?
c. What does her company make?
d. What exactly does she ask the company to send?

Request letters

Customer's letters of request should be answered in a manner that shows you care about their problems and needs. You have an opportunity to build goodwill by personalizing your replies. This in turn tends to make customers loyal to you as a supplier of goods and services. As a result, your responses to request letters can serve as public relations and sales pieces at the same time.

Use the following structure when answering letters of request. Remember that every contact with customers is an opportunity to strengthen their confidence in your ability to meet their needs.

1. Set a friendly, positive tone in the opening paragraph that tells the customer they are valued and appreciated. For new customers you might begin by saying, "We are pleased that you came to us for help..." The long-time customer can be addressed with, "It's good to hear from you again..."

2. Let them know how their request is being handled. If you are responding to an order, tell them when and how the order will reach them. "We will be shipping the cartons UPS. You should receive them by July 15..."

   If they requested information, give them all the data they need. "You will find a complete price list enclosed for all our paper products."Try to anticipate problems or questions the customer may raise and deal with them in your letter. Put yourself in the reader's position and ask what you would need to know from a company.

3. Show confidence in your product or service and invite further business contacts. Your closing should include a message that says, in effect, "We would like your continued business. How can we be of further

service to you?" Your friendly tone is meant to foster goodwill so that the reader remembers not only your product or service but also your attitude toward customers.

Your response to a request letter can work as both a public relations and sales piece for you. Try to convey the message "the customer is our major concern."

Exercise 2 Read the following business letter and answer the questions.

August 17, 2001

Ms. Jean Klein
Tri-Products, Inc.
2502 General Avenue
Flint, Michigan 48553

Dear Ms. Klein:

Thank you for your telephone order of June 6. As you requested, we have ordered the following items:

- 10 packages of white, 3 x 5 pressure-sensitive labels imprinted with your company's name and address
- 5 dozen yellow, 4 x 6 memo pads imprinted with your company's name only

We will ship the memo pads to your attention via UPS by June 15.

Unfortunately, we are presently backordered on pressure-sensitive labels. We anticipate receiving your imprinted labels by June 29 and will ship them by air express at no additional cost. We apologize for the delay.

Thank you for your order-we appreciate your continued business.

Yours truly,

Martin A. Train
Director of Order Department
Mira Office Supplies

1. What is the purpose of this letter?
2. Who is the reader?
3. What does the sender want to say?

Business Writing Simulation

Mrs. Lister asks you to draft a reply, ready for her signature, to the following letter which she has received. She says that you should inquire at the site to check what happened and be tactful in what you write.

April 12, 1999

Snugdale Construction Ltd
Papermill Road
Wolverhampton
WV4 6EP

Dear Sirs:

RE: Newlands Farm Site

Your building site at Newlands Farm is directly behind our house. You may remember that my wife and I objected to the building of the houses which backed onto our garden since we thought they were far too close to our boundary.

Now your workmen have damaged our fence and are refusing to mend it.

They have been most objectionable and shout rude comments at us whenever we go out into our own garden.

What are you going to do?

Yours truly,

Frank Timmins

Frank Timmins

You visit the site and talk with the foreman who says, "Mr. and Mrs. Timmins use binoculars to watch everything we do and if we come near to the boundary they immediately come into their garden to argue with us about building so close. We are only following the plans passed by the Council!"

He adds that the fence had broken because the posts were rotten and that he had said that Snugdale, as a gesture of goodwill, would replace it with a new one as soon as building was completed.

You report to Mrs. Lister who asks you to include in the letter that she will call round herself to see Mr. and Mrs. Timmins to discuss the problems.

Write the letter

Unit 7 Claims and Complaints

Learning Objective:

After studying this unit, you should be able to....

- Understand that the purpose of a claim letter is to convince the reader that you have a legitimate complaint that deserves a desired response.
- Learn that writing a respectful yet firm complaint letter may help you accomplish what you set out to do.

When problems arise

In order to get your problem resolved, put it in writing! A respectful yet firm claim or complaint letter may help you accomplish what you want.

Following are general tips for writing claim and complaint letters. Check what points you consider when writing about a problem.

General tips for claim and complaint letters	*Check*
Try to make sure your letter is sent to the right person or department.	
Try and keep your letter short.	
Be polite as sarcasm or rudeness will not help your cause!	
State what you would like to see happen to resolve the problem.	
Give a reasonable timetable for action to be taken before you will consider other options.	
Keep a copy of letters you write.	

Activity

Pair up and talk about the similarities and differences of claim and complaint letters.

Claim and complaint letters

Claim letters

The more professional the claim letter is, the better the chance you have of receiving positive feedback in your favor. Consider this strategy when writing a claim letter:

Step 1. Identify the product or service
Step 2. Explain the problem
Step 3. Propose a solution
Step 4. End the letter respectfully

Complaint letters

Complaint letters aren't always fun, but sometimes they need to be written. In many cases, if people don't complain, the problem agency at fault (i.e. company or government) won't even know that the problem you and others may have experienced even exists.

<How to write complaint letters>

1. Keep in mind that most errors are unintentional.
2. Be brief.
3. Be honest and straightforward.
4. Maintain a firm but respectful tone and avoid aggressive, accusing language.
5. Send only photocopies of receipts and other documents, retaining all originals.
6. In many cases, you can increase the effectiveness of your letter by getting several others to sign it with you.
7. Voice your feelings in a tactful but firm way. Don't threaten legal action unless you are willing to follow through with it.
8. Include your contact information (name, address, phone number, and e-mail address).

Exercise 1-1 LANGUAGE FOCUS

You can use these expressions to begin your message:

I am writing to complain about ...
I am writing about a problem with ...
I am writing in reference to ...

Note: The first two sentences have a stronger complaining tone than the third.

Write sentences using the expressions above and the phrases below.
Use each expression at least once.

Ex) order # 7214-649
I am writing to complain about order # 7214-649.

a. your latest shipment

____

b. the installation of computer network software

____

c. order # XJ 4311

____

d. the redecoration of our corporate headquarters

____

Exercise 1-2 LANGUAGE FOCUS

You can add extra information about a topic by using expressions such as:

I am writing to complain about order # 7214-649.
(extra information) It arrived yesterday.
I am writing to complain about order # 7212-649, which arrived yesterday.

Add the extra information below in combination with the sentences you wrote in Exercise 1-1.

a. It was delivered this morning.

____

b. It was completed last week.

____

c. It arrived on Friday.

____

d. It was finished yesterday.

____

Exercise 2 LANGUAGE FOCUS

First, say what the problem is:			
We regret to inform you that I am sorry to say that Unfortunately,	the goods were damaged. the shipment arrived late. you sent us the wrong model. the work was unsatisfactory.		
Then give details:			
We ordered TS400 models, but we received TS300. There are cracks in the walls. The plastic casings were scratched in several places. The promised delivery date was January 22, but it arrived February 6.			
If necessary, add any further information:			
We have enclosed Please find enclosed I am attaching	a copy a photocopy photographs	of the	order. shipping order. damage. work.

We can combine the sentences above like this:

Ex) I am sorry to say that the goods were damaged. The plastic casings were scratched in several places. We have enclosed photographs of the damage.

Create three other situations by combining the problem, details, and further information as in the example.

a. ____

____

____

b. ____

____

____

c. ____

____

____

Answering Complaint Letters

"Good News" Response to Complaint Letters

•General guidelines for answering complaint letters include:

▷Be prompt and courteous.

▷Be sure that your responses are complete-that they include all needed information.

▷If you are giving some positive and some negative responses, give the positive responses first. Try to emphasis what you CAN do-not what you CAN'T do.

•The body of the very simplest "good news" letter is often just two paragraphs. In these letters the "good news" is given in the opening. Any "call for action" and your marketing statement are put in the second paragraph. Simple details, such as when a package will be shipped, can be put either at the end of the first paragraph or the beginning of the second.

•More complex "good news" letters would include those where conditions must be met in order for the request to be granted, or those letters where only part of the request can be granted. These letters are usually three or more paragraphs in length.

"Good News" letter format

1. **Opening paragraph:** Tell the good news. In this paragraph you may want to include a sentence showing appreciation towards the reader. In letters giving both positive and negative responses to a letter, think about giving only the positive responses in the opening-what you can do. Explain what you can't do at the end of the middle part of the letter.

2. **Middle:** Give the details. Specific details are given in the middle paragraphs of your letter. In only the very simplest "good news" letters this information can be put at the end of the opening paragraph.
   - This part of the letter is where you give information about how the request will be granted or the conditions that must be met before you can grant the request.
   - If several questions have been asked, make sure you answer each question-possibly in separate paragraphs. If your responses to all questions are positive, answer them in the order asked. If you are giving some positive and some negative responses, give the positive responses first.
   - Finish this section by telling the reader any requests you cannot satisfy, along with a reason why. Try to tell the reason why before you tell what you can't do.

3. **Closing paragraph:** Your "CALL FOR ACTION." Restate, in general, any action needed from your reader for you to grant the request. If a time element is important, give specific dates. Because you are giving a positive response, you should try to include a marketing statement in your closing.

"Bad News" Response to Complaint Letters

- Don't deliver the bad news in the opening paragraph.
- Always try to tell what you **CAN** do before you say what you **CAN'T** do.
- Explain the **WHY** before you deliver the bad news. For many readers, once they see the NO they don't pay attention to the reason why.
- Remember that a major goal is to maintain a positive relationship with the reader. Do whatever you can to help the reader understand and accept your message.
- When you are through writing the letter, make sure the message that you cannot grant the request is clear.

"Bad News" letter format (usually three or four paragraphs)

1. **Opening paragraph:** Show appreciation for the reader, but don't deliver the "bad news" here. This is your buffer paragraph.

2. **Middle:** Give the reasons why you cannot grant the request-then deliver the bad news. This is the hard part of the letter to write. Remember that your goal is to help the reader understand and accept your decision. Try to state the refusal in a positive way. Sometimes you can soften the blow by implying the bad news and still leave a clear understanding with the reader.

3. **Closing paragraph:** If at all possible, state something you CAN do for the reader in the closing. In any case, provide the reader with a suggested action to remedy the situation. Close with a positive statement.

Exercise 3-1

Fill in the blanks, using the words below.

inspect	items	insure	replacement

a. Please send us the correct __________________ by January 14.

b. Please __________________ that future shipments arrive on time.

c. Please send us the __________________ goods as soon as possible.

d. Please send someone to __________________ the building immediately.

Exercise 3-2

Talk to a partner. Match the solutions above to the situations in Exercise 2.

Exercise 4-1

Look at this advice for responding to a complaint. Fill in the blanks, using the words below.

give	write	thank	refer	say

a. __________________ your customer for writing to you.

b. __________________ to the problem and apologize.

c. __________________ an explanation for the problem, if possible.

d. __________________ how you are going to help the customer.

e. __________________ a polite conclusion.

Exercise 4-2

The sentences below are from a letter responding to a complaint.
Put them in the correct order.

Number	
	Dear Mr. Watanabe,
☐	We will send you the correct items free of charge.
☐	We are sorry to hear that you received the wrong order.
☐	Once again, please accept our apologies for the inconvenience, and we look forward to serving you again in the future.
☐	Thank you for your letter dated October 26 concerning your recent order.
☐	Apparently, this was caused by a processing error.
	Sincerely, *Vince Picardo* Vince Picardo

Exercise 4-3

Write the phrases in the letter in Exercise 4-2 which have the same meaning as these expressions.

a. regarding ______________________

b. we regret to learn ______________________

c. this was the result of ______________________

d. at no extra cost ______________________

e. we apologize ______________________

Exercise 4-4

Rewrite the letter in Exercise 4-2, using the expressions in Exercise 4-3 and this information.

- Ms. Pang
- e-mail / May 10 / the installation of computer accounting software
- the installation was unsatisfactory
- was caused by a fault in the CD
- will send a replacement CD immediately

Business Writing Simulation

Suppose you are writing a complaint letter to a service provider. Write a letter using the format given below.

<Basic format>

Your address
Your city, state, and zip code
Date

Name of contact person, if available
Title, if available
Consumer complaint division (If you have no specific contact)
Company name
Street address
City, state, and zip code

RE: (account number, if applicable)

Dear (contact person):

On (date), I (bought, leased, rented, or had repaired) a (name of the product, with serial or model number or service performed) at (location, date, and other important details of the transaction).

Unfortunately, your product (or service) has not performed well (or the service was inadequate) because (state the problem). I am disappointed because (explain the problem: for example, the product does not work properly, the service was not performed correctly, I was billed the wrong amount, something was not disclosed clearly or was misrepresented, etc.).

To resolve the problem, I would appreciate your (state the specific action you want–money back, charge card credit, repair, exchange, etc.) Enclosed are copies (do not send originals) of my records (include receipts, guarantees, warranties, canceled checks, contracts, model and serial numbers, and any other documents).

I look forward to your reply and a resolution to my problem and will wait until (set a time limit) before seeking help from a consumer protection agency or the Better Business Bureau. Please contact me at the above address or by phone at (home and/or office numbers with area code).

Sincerely,

Your name

<Writing worksheet>

Unit 8 Sales Letters

Learning Objective:

After studying this unit, you should be able to....

- Learn how to write effective sales letters.
- Write a sales letter that is specific, directed to the right audience, appealing to readers' needs, and informative.

Questionnaire : What you should consider in a sales letter

When writing a sales letter, what do you think you should consider among the factors below? Choose two out of each section.

INGREDIENTS OF AN EFFECTIVE SALES LETTER	*Check*
1. What are the three most important ingredients of a sales letter?	
2. How can I boost my credibility in the letter?	
3. When should I personalize a letter?	
4. Do I need an order form?	
5. Is there anything else that boosts response?	
WRITING AND FORMATTING THE SALES LETTER AND ENVELOPE	*Check*
1. How long should my sales letter be?	
2. If I'm·sending a brochure, do I need to include a sales letter too?	
3. What font style and font size should I use?	
4. Should I incorporate a photo and fancy graphics into my letter?	
5. Do I need "teaser copy" on the envelope?	
6. How should I address the envelope?	
7. Should I use stamps, metered postage, or a permit number on the envelope?	
SALES LETTERS VIA E-MAIL AND ON THE WEB	*Check*
1. Do the same principles apply to sales letters sent by e-mail?	
2. How do I find lists of addresses to send e-mail sales letters to?	
3. Does it make sense to post a sales letter on a web site?	

Activity

Pair up and discuss the questions you chose above.

Questionnaire : How can I write an effective sales letter?

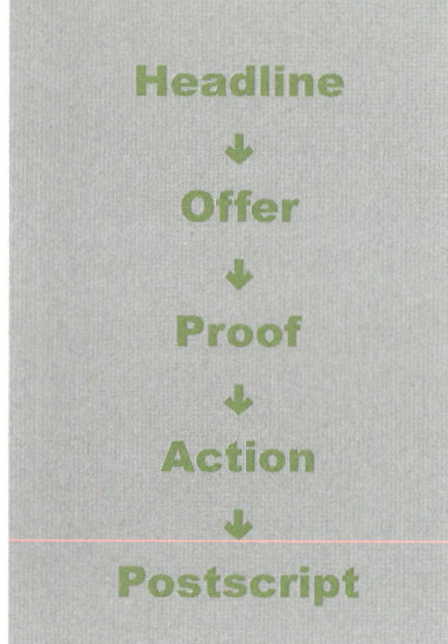

Sales letters can be extremely powerful; marketing studies show that they outperform other direct mail formats such as brochures and postcards. But before you get to see how effective sales letters are for yourself, you have to write one. Here's how to write a sales letter that will wow your readers and persuade them to buy your product or service.

Exercise 1 Read the following and try to identify which parts of a sales letter they belong to.

____

This part needs to get the reader's attention. Its job is to make the reader want to know more (and actually read your sales letter). Make sure it makes a specific promise that relates to your prospects' needs or interests. If, for instance, you offer domestic cleaning services, don't use a saying such as "Want Cleaning Services?" in your sales letter. Instead use something such as "We Do It For You, So You Don't Have To!"

____

In this part you need to tell your prospective customers what you're offering them first. The trick is that you have to make them want your product or service. So think like a prospective customer or client when you're writing this section of your sales letter and answer the question, "What's in it for me?" In other words, what are the benefits to the customer of making this purchase?

For instance, "For less than $100 you can have your entire home clean and sparkling without enduring the nasty stink of chemical cleaners."

Don't be afraid to expand on the benefits of your product or service. People who are interested will read the details. Use bullet points or arrows where appropriate to make your sales letter easier to read.

And remember that your sales letter does not have to be limited to a single page. You can send out an eight page one if you want! What's the best length? That will depend on your target market and your product or service. Many businesses that use sales letters find that longer sales letter are more effective. If this is your first, try to limit the length.

____

Another thing you need to do in the body of the sales letter is assure your readers that they will be satisfied with their purchase. Testimonials (statements of satisfaction from past customers) are an excellent way of doing this. Or offer your reader a "fail-safe," such as a money-back guarantee, or entice them with a free trial offer.

____

The most important thing that you need to do in the body of your sales letter, of course, is persuade the reader to act. First, be sure you come right out and say what you want the reader of your letter to do, whether it's to call you or come into your store. Second, make it easy for your customer to act. Set a deadline for the expiration of your offer, throw in a free gift, or, if it's appropriate, make a moral plea.

____

You've asked your reader once. Hopefully he's thinking about it. Add a P.S. to your sales letter to light a fire under your customer and get him to act RIGHT NOW. Use a carrot such as throwing in an additional bonus (such as, "If you act right now, you'll also receive..."), or a stick, such as reminding the customer that quantities are limited or that the price will only be as stated in the offer for a certain period of time (set a date).

The 12 Steps of Creating a Winning Sales Letter

1. Get Their Attention

Assuming the reader has opened your envelope, the next step is to get their attention, The opening headline is the first thing that your reader will look at. If it doesn't catch their attention you can kiss your letter goodbye. People have a very short attention span and usually sort their mail over the wastebasket. If the headline doesn't call out to them and pique their interest, they will just stop and throw your letter away.

The following are three headline-generating templates that are proven to get attention.

"HOW TO ________________"
People love to know how to do things.

"SECRETS OF ________________ REVEALED!"
People always want to know "insider secrets." We love to know things that other people don't.

"WARNING: DON'T EVEN THINK OF ________________ UNTIL YOU ________________."
Remember that people are motivated by fear of loss more than the promise of gain. The word "warning" demands attention, and when it is combined with something of interest to the reader, it is a very powerful headline.

Exercise 2 Write a headline for one of your company's products using the patterns on the previous page.

2. Identify the Problem

Now that you have your reader's attention you need to gain their interest by spelling out their problem and how it feels to have that problem. The reader should say to himself, "Yeah, that's exactly how I feel" when they read your letter. In fact, you shouldn't stop there. Pretend that it's an open wound that you're rubbing salt into.

This technique is called "problem - agitate." For example, if you were selling garage door openers, you might agitate the problem by telling a short story about what happens when it doesn't work.

Example

"There's nothing worse than getting home in the evening and not having your garage door open. It's dark outside and after tripping on the porch step you search for your front door key. Finally, you find it only to scratch your new front door up trying to find the keyhole. Exhausted, you get inside and plop down on the couch just when you remember your car is still running in your driveway...."

In this scenario the problem was a faulty garage door opener and the agitation is all the terrible things that happen because of the faulty garage door opener.

3. Provide the Solution

Now that you've built your reader's interest by making them feel pain, it's time to provide the solution. This is the part of the sales letter where you boldly stake your claim that you can solve the reader's problem. In this section you will introduce yourself, your product, and/or your service. Relieve the reader's mind by telling them that there's no need to struggle with all their problems because your product or service will solve it for them.

4. Present your Credentials

In most cases, after you have introduced yourself and your product or service your reader is thinking, "Yeah, sure he can fix my problem. That's what they all say." So now it's important to hit them right away with the reason why you can be trusted.

List your credentials, including any one of the following:

1. Successful case studies
2. Prestigious companies (or people) you have done business with
3. The length of time you've been in your field of expertise
4. Conferences where you have spoken
5. Important awards or recognitions

Your reader should get the impression after reading this section that "you've been there and done that" with great success and that the reader can expect the same results.

5. Show the Benefits

Now it's time to tell the reader how they will personally benefit from your product or service. Don't make the common mistake of telling all about the features of your product without talking about the benefits.

Think about the obvious benefits and the hidden benefits that people won't naturally think of. For example, a hot tub not only soothes and relaxes your muscles but it also gives you an opportunity to talk to your spouse without interruptions. The hidden benefit is greater communication with your spouse and ultimately a better marriage!

Bullet points each benefit to make it easier to read. Think about every possible benefit your reader may derive from your product or service. In many cases, people will buy a product or service based on only one of the benefits you list.

6. Give Social Proof

After you've presented all your benefits, the reader will again begin to doubt you even though they secretly want all your claimed benefits to be true. To build your credibility and believability, present your reader with testimonials from satisfied customers.

Testimonials are powerful selling tools that prove your claims to be true. To make your testimonial even more powerful, include pictures of your customers with their names and addresses (at least the city and state).

You might even ask if you can use their phone number. Most readers won't call, but it is a powerful statement to include customers' complete contact information. It demonstrates that both you and the testimonials are real.

7. Make Your Offer

Your offer is the most important part of your sales letter. A great offer can overcome mediocre writing, but great writing cannot overcome a mediocre offer. Your offer should be irresistible. You want your readers to say to themselves, "I'd be stupid not to take advantage of this deal."

Your offer can come in many different formats. The best offers are usually an attractive combination of price, terms, and free gifts. For example, if you were selling a car your offer might be a discounted retail price, low interest rate, and a free year of gas.

Hint: When developing your offer you should always try to raise the value of your offer by adding on products or services rather than lowering your price. Include vivid explanations of the benefits of the additional products or services you are offering in order to raise the perceived value of your offer.

8. Give a Guarantee

To make your offer even more irresistible you need to take all the risk out of the purchase. Remember that people have a built-in fear that they are going to get ripped off. How many times have you purchased a product and got stuck with it because the merchant wouldn't give your money back? Give the absolute strongest guarantee you are able to give.

Most businesses already have a strong guarantee and don't hold it up and trumpet it for fear that a lot of people would take them up on it. That's simply doesn't happen. When was the last time you asked for a full refund on something?

Here is an example of a guarantee for an online course:

* * "**100%, No Questions Asked, Take-It-To-The-Bank Guarantee**" * *

I personally guarantee if you make a diligent effort to use just a few of the techniques in this course, you'll produce at least $4,490 profit in the next 12 months. That's right, $4,490 extra profit you never would have seen without this course. If you don't, I'll refund the entire cost of the course to you.

Actually, you get double protection. Here's how. At any time during the 12 months, if you sincerely feel I fell short in any way on delivering everything I promised, I'll be happy to give you a complete refund. Even if it's on the last day of the twelfth month!

This guarantee extends for an entire year and they will receive specific benefits (in this case it's money). It they don't get what they expect, they get their money back with no questions asked. This virtually eliminates all the risk for the buyer.

9. Inject Scarcity

Most people take their time responding to offers, even when they are irresistible. There are many reasons why people procrastinate on investing in a solution. The following are just a few:

- **They don't feel enough pain to make a change.**
- **They are too busy and just forget.**
- **They don't feel that the perceived value outweighs your asking price.**
- **They are just plain lazy.**

When people think there is a scarce supply of something they need, they usually rush to get some of it. You can create a feeling of scarcity by telling your reader that either the quantity is in limited supply or that your offer is valid for only a limited time period.

Your offer could sound something like this:

"If you purchase by (future date), you will get the entire set of free bonuses."

Or

"Our supply is limited to only 50 (product or service) and will be sent to you on a 'first come, first served' basis. After they are gone there won't be any more available."

Or

"This offer is only good until (future date) after which the (product or service) will return to its original price."

10. Call to action

Do not assume that your reader knows what to do to receive the benefits from your offer. You must spell out how to make the order in very clear and concise language. Whether it's picking up the phone and making the call, filling out an order form, or faxing the order form to your office, you must tell them exactly how to order from you.

Your call to action must be "action-oriented." You can do this using words like "Pick Up the Phone and Call Now!" or "Tear Off the Order Form and Send It In Today!" or "Come to Our Store by Friday and ..." Be explicit and succinct in your instructions.

Plant your call to action throughout your letter. If you are asking the reader to call your free information line, then perhaps some of the testimonials might say, "When I called their free information line" or in your offer you might say, "When you call our free information line..." Then when you give the call to action at the end of the letter, people won't be surprised or confused. It will be consistent with what you said all throughout your letter.

11. Give a Warning

A good sales letter will continue to build emotion, right up to the very end. In fact, your letter should continue to build emotion even after your call to action. Using the "risk of loss" strategy, tell the reader what would happen if they didn't take advantage of your offer. Perhaps they would continue to:

- Struggle day to day to make ends meet
- Work too hard just to get a few customers
- Lose the opportunity to receive all your valuable bonuses
- Keep getting what they've always got
- Watch other companies get all the business

Try to paint a graphic picture in the mind of the reader about the consequences of not taking action now.

Remind them just how terrible their current state is and that it just doesn't have to be that way.

Exercise 3

Thinking of one of your company's products, write a warning message that calls for an action.

Your product: ____________

Warning message:

____

____

____

____

12. Close with a Reminder

Always include a postscript (P.S.). Believe it or not, your P.S. is the third most read element of your sales letter. In your postscript you want to remind them of your irresistible offer. If you've used scarcity in your sales letter, include your call to action and then remind them of the limited time (or quantity) of the offer. It sounds like a simple step, but postscripts get noticed.

Exercise 4 Pair up. Following the tips above, create a P.S. message for your letter.

Business Writing Simulation

Write your own sales letter using the samples below for help.

<Sample #1>

[Date]

[Mr./Mrs./Ms./Dr.] [Customer's Full Name]
[Title]
[Company Name]
[Address] [City], [State] [Zip/Postal Code]

Dear [Mr./Mrs./Ms./Dr.] [Customer's Last Name]:

Don't lose this letter, or you'll lose your free gift!

[Name of Your Store] is having our [Name of the Sale] Sale, and we want you to be there for outstanding savings on everything in the store.

And a FREE gift everyone will love.

Beginning on [First Day of the Sale, Including Month, Day and Year] and ending on [Customer's Last Day of the Sale, Including Month, Day and Year], [Name of Your Store] will have huge discounts, up to [Highest Percentage Customer Can Save During Sale]% on items like these:

[Highest Percentage Customer Can Save During Sale]% off all [First Type of Product On Sale at the Highest Discount]. Or [Highest Percentage Customer Can Save During Sale]% off all [Second Type of Product On Sale at the Highest Discount]. Or [Highest Percentage Customer Can Save During Sale]% off all [Third Type of Product On Sale at the Highest Discount].

And not only will you save, but if you bring in this letter during the [Name of the Sale] Sale, we'll also give you a [Name of the Free Gift], absolutely free.

Mark your calendar now for the [Name of the Sale] Sale: [First Day of the Sale, Including Month, Day and Year] - [Customer's Last Day of the Sale, Including Month, Day and Year]. Come to the sale early, and don't forget to bring this letter because our [Name of the Free Gift] supplies are limited.

And there's no telling when we'll run out.

Sincerely,

[Your Name]
[Your Title]
[Your Company Name]

P.S. Tape this letter to your door-mail it to yourself-put it in the glove compartment of your car-just don't lose it or you won't get [Name of the Free Gift] for free.

<Sample #2>

[Date]

[Mr./Mrs./Ms./Dr.] [Customer's Full Name]
[Title]
[Company Name]
[Address] [City], [State] [Zip/Postal Code]

Dear [Mr./Mrs./Ms./Dr.] [Customer's Last Name]:

NEW! We've just received a shipment of thousands of new [Name of the Product] and we need to get them moving!
So we've knocked off the price by [Percentage Customer Can Save By Ordering the Product from You]%–you can get your [Name of the Product] right now for just $[Price of Product].

We’ve never offered [Name of the Product] before, and we don’t know exactly how you will respond to them. That's why we're offering them at such a low price.

We'll keep this low price for as long as we can, but if the demand is high, we'll be forced to raise our prices.

Sorry, but those are the laws of supply and demand.

So order yours now, while we’re still offering this incredible introductory price–just $[Price of Product]. Call [Phone Number Customers Call to Place Orders, Preferably a Toll-free or 800 Number] right now and give our brand new [Name of the Product] a try.

Sincerely,

[Your Name]
[Your Title]
[Your Company Name]

P.S. Don't forget about our return policy. Return any product to us within [Number of Days the Guarantee Lasts] days and we'll refund your purchase price.

<Writing worksheet>

Unit 9 Using E-mail

Learning Objective:

After studying this unit, you should be able to....

- Explain instances when sending e-mail is necessary and appropriate.
- Create an e-mail subject line that can accurately describe the content of the message.

Questionnaire : Evaluate your understanding of e-mail writing

	True	*False*
1. Because e-mail is intended-and expected-to be a quick, informal means of communication, the usual rules of grammar, punctuation, and style don't apply.		
2. You can enhance the readability and impact of your e-mail message by using all uppercase (or all lowercase) letters.		
3. Short sentences indicate intellectual weakness. You are certain to impress readers by writing long, heavily punctuated sentences.		
4. Always save the best stuff for the end. If you reveal the most important information up front, the reader will have no incentive to finish reading your document.		
5. Electronic writing is fundamentally different from traditional writing.		

Check the answers on page 104 to find out how well you understand e-mail writing.

5 False: You are well on your way to becoming an effective electronic writer.

4 False: Remember, good writing is good writing, regardless of whether it's produced on paper or on a screen.

2-3 False: Before you begin writing, focus on your goal. As a writer, your primary job is to persuade the reader. It's hard to persuade someone who can't understand what you are saying.

1 False: A comprehensive grammar and punctuation review may be a good idea.

Activity

Pair up and compare your answers to the above questionnaire.

E-mail Writing Tips

- E-mail is much less formal than a written letter. E-mails are usually short and concise.
- If you are writing to someone you don't know, a simple "Hello" is adequate. Using a salutation, such as "Dear Mr. Smith," is too formal.
- When writing to someone you know well, feel free to write as if you are speaking to the person.
- Use abbreviated verb forms (he's, we're, she'd, etc.).
- Include a telephone number with the signature of the e-mail. This will give the recipient the chance to telephone if necessary.
- It is not necessary to include your e-mail address as the recipient can just reply to the e-mail.
- When replying to an e-mail, delete as much of the original e-mail as possible. Only leave the sections of text that are related to your reply. This will save your reader time when reading your e-mail.

Examples of e-mails

Example 1 Formal

Hello,

I read on your web site that you offer music CD copying for large quantities of CDs. I'd like to inquire about the procedures involved in these services. Are the files transferred online, or are the titles sent by CD to you by standard mail? How long does it usually take to produce approximately 500 copies? Are there any discounts on such a large quantity?

Thank you for taking the time to answer my questions. I look forward to your response.

Jack Finley
Sales Manager, Young Talent Inc.
(709) 567 - 3498

Example 2 Informal

Hi Tom,

Listen, we've been working on the Smith account and I was wondering if you could give me a hand. I need some inside information on recent developments over there.

Do you think you could pass on any information you might have?

Thanks,

Peter

Account Manager, Tri-State Accounting
(698) 345 - 7843

Dangers of using e-mail for all of your business communications:

1. **Misunderstandings** : Without hearing your voice or seeing your facial expressions, it is difficult to discern tone, meaning, and emphasis. A person can interpret your written message differently than if he was talking to you on the phone or in person.
2. **Decisions can be delayed** : If someone needs more information from you to make a decision, he has to ask questions. You can spend a lot of time going back and forth with e-mail. Contrast that with picking up the phone and handling the issues in a conversation.
3. **A sloppy image** : How many e-mails do you read that have typos and other errors? Because people are replying to messages so quickly (sometimes before thinking) and doing it while other things are going on, words are left out or misspelled and sometimes e-mails just don't make sense!
4. **Your message gets lost** : If you don't have a compelling subject line, your e-mail may not even get opened. And, if it does get opened and it is lengthy with long paragraphs, many readers will just stop reading.

Since work involves working with people and getting things done through people, you have to build relationships. You have to interact, get to know someone, and build trust. If you have become too dependant on e-mail your relationships may suffer as a result.

Exercise 1 Pair up and answer the following questions with your partner.

1. Which one below indicates an e-mail address?
   A) www.gte.com/email
   B) http://jsmart.edu
   C) jsmart@fast.com
   D) D:/jsmart/email

2. Which software below is an e-mail client?
   A) Windows 98
   B) Internet Explorer
   C) MS-Office
   D) Outlook

3. How can you send e-mail to more than one recipient at the same time?
   A) By sending an e-mail with a notice to be forwarded to the rest of the recipients
   B) This is not possible at this time in Outlook Express
   C) By adding a second recipient in the "Cc" field
   D) By adding all recipients' e-mail addresses in the "To" field

4. Can your computer get infected by a virus via e-mail?
   A) No
   B) Only if the e-mail has an attached executable program
   C) Yes
   D) Only if the e-mail has an infected Word document attached

5. How can you organize your e-mail in the folders of your choice?
   A) By creating your own folders under File/Folder/New
   B) By using Windows Explorer and creating new folders
   C) By downloading folders via your address book
   D) None of the above

6. Why do some e-mail addresses complete automatically as you type them and others do not?
   A) The AutoComplete works only for addresses not stored into your address book
   B) The AutoComplete works only for addresses inside Microsoft Outlook
   C) The AutoComplete works only for addresses already stored into your address book
   D) The AutoComplete works only when you reply to an e-mail

7. How can you set your Outlook Express to always spell check before sending?
   A) By pressing the F7 key
   B) By going to Tools/Options/Spelling
   C) By highlighting the text and using the Spell Checker
   D) You cannot do this at this time

8. If you enclose a graphic with your e-mail you need to make sure that:
   A) Your recipient has a color printer
   B) You have enough memory in your computer to send it
   C) Your recipient is close by in order to avoid data corruption
   D) Your recipient's client e-mail software can display graphics

9. Your e-mail client has been open for a while. Is the information displayed up-to-date?
   A) It is always up-to-date
   B) You need to restart your client in order to receive any new e-mail
   C) Not necessarily. You need to click on "Send and Receive" to check for new mail
   D) The client checks the server every ten minutes for new e-mail, so you have to wait

E-mail Templates

Friendlier, less structured e-mail template

Essential elements:

- Subject line
- Who (target audience)
- What
- When / by when (deadlines)
- Why (purpose)
- Benefits (to target audience)
- Action requested
- Signature block

Benefits of e-mail template #1:

- Clear subject line enables relevant audience to find and open messages that concern issues they consider important
- Provides room to be friendlier and more engaging
- Flexibility for the writer

Drawbacks of e-mail template #1:

- Easier to forget, drop, or gloss over individual essential elements, especially if the writer does not have a strong track record of clear, concise communications
- Harder for the reader to scan for information she/he considers most relevant
- "Providing room to be friendlier" can make it tempting to run on and pad sentences with more wording than is needed

More formally structured e-mail template

Essential elements:

- Subject line
- Who (target audience)
- Purpose
- Background
- What
- When / by when (deadlines)
- Why (purpose)
- Benefits (to target audience)
- Action requested
- Signature block

Benefits of e-mail template #2:

- Good practice in writing messages that include all key elements that a reader may want
- Can help the writer enforce self-discipline in writing without verbiage
- Easy for the reader to quickly scan for relevant information

Drawbacks of e-mail template #2:

- Can feel overly structured, awkward for the writer
- May seem unfriendly and impersonal to the reader

Exercise 2

Complete the following chart with information found in the e-mail below.

Items	*Content from e-mail*
Subject line	
Who (target audience)	
Purpose	
Background	
What	
When / by when (deadlines)	
Why (purpose)	
Benefits (to target audience)	
Action requested	
Signature block	

From: Theresa M. Regan <tregan@MIT.EDU>
Date: Wed., 22 Sept. 2004 09:28:37 -0400
To: spamscreen-users@mit.edu
Subject: Spam Screening @ MIT - auto purging extended to 21 days

Good Morning,

Presently, your e-mail account is set to auto-purge e-mail messages older than 14 days from your "Spamscreen" folder on the MIT mail system.

IS&T wishes to alert you to an upcoming change in this service effective Monday, October 4th, 2004. We will extend the age of messages to be purged from your "Spamscreen" folder from 14 days or greater to 21 days or greater as of this date. This change is necessitated by another important upcoming enhancement in our service. Shortly, we will begin automatically creating "Spamscreen" folders for all new accounts. We are increasing the age of messages to be purged by one week to allow additional time for new MIT colleagues and students to acclimate to our environment and this important service.

More information about our service is available at:

<http://web.mit.edu/ist/services/email/nospam/>

Below, please find the community-wide announcement which includes more complete information about these enhancements. If you have additional comments, suggestions, or questions, please feel free to contact the IS&T Computing Help Desk <computing-help@mit.edu> or me.

Cheers,

Theresa

Business Writing Simulation

Suppose you are writing an e-mail to someone. Write an e-mail for each situation given below. Use the techniques you have learned.

1. Fan e-mail to an entertainment or sports personality
2. Political e-mail to a national or international organization
3. E-mail of praise or complaint
4. E-mail requesting a pay raise

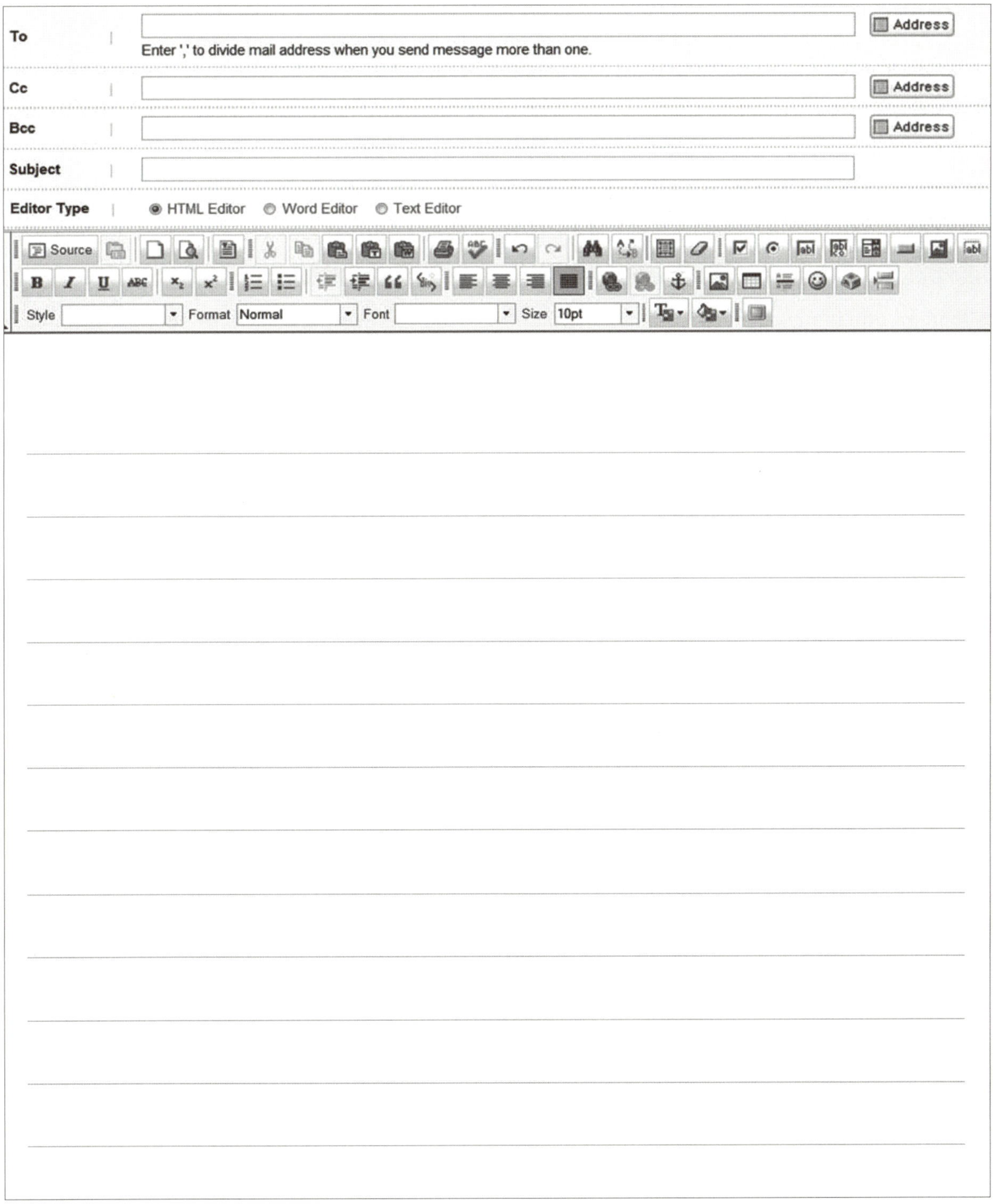

To | Address
Enter ',' to divide mail address when you send message more than one.
Cc | Address
Bcc | Address
Subject |
Editor Type | HTML Editor Word Editor Text Editor
Source
Style Format Normal Font Size 10pt

Unit 10 E-mail Etiquette

Learning Objective:

After studying this unit, you should be able to....

- Explain how to write effective e-mails.
- Understand the necessity of e-mail etiquette and understand its rules.

Questionnaire : Writing for International Audiences

You can send an e-mail message across the continent or around the world as easily as you can communicate with your colleagues in the next cubicle. Check whether you are prepared for the cultural challenges of international electronic communication with the following statements.

	Yes	No
1. Fundamentally, there is no difference between international and domestic e-mail.		
2. You don't have to worry about language barriers. English is, after all, the international language of commerce.		
3. International e-mails call for more detailed and specific information than do local e-mails.		
4. All speakers of any given language are culturally similar.		
5. When e-mailing a colleague in another country, it is all right to use technical jargon, acronyms, and abbreviations.		

Activity

Pair up and discuss each point above with your partner.

Grabbing the Reader s Attention: The Lead

To maximize the impact of any written document—electronic or traditional—you must start strong. The lead—beginning with the first word of the first sentence and ending at the conclusion of the first paragraph—is the writer's best, and sometimes only, opportunity to grab the reader's attention.

The Lead's Roles

- The lead structures your message. The reader has no doubt why you have written it or whether to continue reading.
- The lead delivers the document's most important, compelling information right up front, often in the form of a conclusion.
- The lead summarizes what is to come later in the document.
- The lead captures-and holds-the reader's attention.

Sample Leads

Weak Lead

Of LLF & Associates' 2,500 employees, approximately 2,000 are using the company's e-mail system on a regular basis. The problem is that many of the 2,000 people enjoying the company's e-mail are using it for personal correspondence. Management is aware this is going on and wants it stopped. As of January 1, the e-mail system of LLF & Associates is reserved for business use only. Any employee caught using it for personal reasons will be put on probation. Three violations of the new e-mail policy will result in termination.

Analysis: This weak lead contains too much unnecessary and secondary information, all of which appears at the beginning of the paragraph. The reader does not learn until the final three sentences that the company is instituting a tough new e-mail policy.

Revised Lead

Effective January 1, personal use of LLF & Associates' corporate e-mail is prohibited. Employees who violate this e-mail policy by making personal use of the system will be put on immediate probation. Three violations will result in termination.

Analysis: This strong lead tells readers what they need to know. A busy reader can grasp the message's meaning immediately.

Exercise 1

After reading the following lead of an e-mail and its analysis, revise the lead to make it stronger.

Weak Lead

> This is a response I have written to Gloria, who recently shared her thoughts about her concerns for our association and our board. I think she has raised important issues that we must address. I send it to you because Tim and I believe we absolutely need a strategic planning session no later than December.

Analysis: The writer wastes valuable time describing the e-mail message to the reader (This is a response I have written...; I send it to you because...) rather than simply delivering the message. A well-written message should be strong enough to stand alone without any introduction.

Revised Lead

E-mail Etiquette Rules

There are many etiquette guides and many different etiquette rules. Some rules will differ according to the nature of your business and the corporate culture. Below are some of the most important e-mail etiquette rules.

1. Be concise and get to the point.

Do not make an e-mail longer than it needs to be. Remember that reading an e-mail is harder than reading printed communications and a long e-mail can be very discouraging to read.

2. Answer all questions, and pre-empt further questions.

An e-mail reply must answer all questions and pre-empt further questions. If you do not answer all the questions in the original e-mail, you will receive further e-mails regarding the unanswered questions, which will not only waste your time and your customer's time but also cause considerable frustration. Moreover, if you are able to pre-empt relevant questions, your customer will be grateful and impressed with your efficient and thoughtful customer service.

3. Use proper spelling, grammar, and punctuation.

This is important not only because improper spelling, grammar, and punctuation give a bad impression of your company, but also because it helps to convey the message properly.

4. Make it personal.

E-mail should be personally addressed and include customized content. For this reason, auto replies are usually not very effective.

5. Use templates for frequently used responses.

Some questions you get over and over again, such as directions to your office or how to subscribe to your newsletter. Save these texts as response templates and paste these into your message when you need them.

6. Answer swiftly.

Customers send an e-mail because they wish to receive a quick response. If they did not want a quick response, they would send a letter or a fax. Therefore, each e-mail should be replied to within at least 24 hours, and preferably within the same working day. If the e-mail is complicated, just send an e-mail back saying that you have received it and that you will get back to them as soon as possible.

7. Do not attach unnecessary files.

By sending large attachments you can annoy customers and even bring down their e-mail system. Wherever possible, try to compress attachments and only send attachments when they are productive.

8. Use proper structure and layout.

Since reading from a screen is more difficult than reading from paper, the structure and layout is very important for e-mail messages. Use short paragraphs and blank lines between each paragraph. When making points, number them or mark each point as separate to keep it simple.

9. Do not overuse the high priority option.

We all know the story of the boy who cried wolf. If you overuse the high priority option, it will not be effective when you really need it.

10. Do not write in CAPITALS.

IF YOU WRITE IN CAPITALS IT SEEMS AS IF YOU ARE SHOUTING. This can be highly annoying and might trigger an unwanted response in the form of a flame mail.

11. Don't leave out the message thread.

When you reply to an e-mail, you must include the original mail in your reply. In other words click "Reply" instead of "New Mail." If you receive many e-mails, you obviously cannot remember each individual e-mail. Leaving the thread might take a fraction longer in download time, but it will save the recipient much more time and frustration from looking for the related e-mails in their inbox!

12. Add disclaimers to your e-mails.

It is important to add disclaimers to your internal and external e-mails since this can help protect your company from liability. Consider the following scenario: an employee accidentally forwards a virus to a customer by e-mail. The customer decides to sue your company for damages. If you add a disclaimer at the bottom of every external e-mail, saying that the recipient must check each e-mail for viruses and that your company cannot be held liable for any transmitted viruses, this will surely be of help to you in court.

13. Read the e-mail before you send it.

A lot of people don't bother to read an e-mail before they send it out, as can be seen from the many spelling and grammar mistakes contained in e-mails. Apart from this, reading your e-mail through the eyes of the recipient will help you send a more effective message and avoid misunderstandings and inappropriate comments.

14. Do not overuse Reply to All.

Only use Reply to All if you really need your message to be seen by each person who received the original message.

15. When doing a mass mailing, use the Bcc: field or do a mail merge.

When sending an e-mail as a mass mailing, some people place all the email addresses in the To: field. There are two drawbacks to this practice: (1) the recipient knows that you have sent the same message to a large number of recipients, and (2) you are publicizing someone else's e-mail address without their permission. One way to get around this is to place all addresses in the Bcc: field.

16. Take care with abbreviations and emoticons.

In business e-mails, try not to use abbreviations such as BTW (by the way) and LOL (laugh out loud). The recipient might not be aware of the meanings of the abbreviations, and in business e-mails these are generally not appropriate. The same goes for emoticons, such as the smiley :-).

17. Be careful with formatting.

The sender might not be able to view formatting, or might see different fonts than you had intended. When using colors, use a color that is easy to read on the background.

18. Do not forward chain letters.

Do not forward chain letters. Just delete the letters as soon as you receive them.

19. Do not request delivery and read receipts.

This will almost always annoy your recipient before he or she has even read your message. Besides, it usually does not work anyway since the recipient could have blocked that function, or his/her software might not support it, so what is the use of using it? If you want to know whether an e-mail was received, it is better to ask the recipient to let you know if it was received.

20. Do not copy a message or attachment without permission.

Do not copy a message or attachment belonging to another user without permission of the originator. If you do not ask permission first, you might be infringing on copyright laws.

21. Do not use e-mail to discuss confidential information.

Sending an e-mail is like sending a postcard. If you don't want your e-mail to be displayed on a bulletin board, don't send it.

22. Use a meaningful subject.

Try to use a subject that is meaningful to the recipient as well as yourself. For instance, when you send an e-mail to a company requesting information about a product, it is better to mention the actual name of the product, e.g. "Product A information" than to just say "product information" or the company's name in the subject.

23. Use active instead of passive.

Try to use the active voice of a verb wherever possible. For instance, "We will process your order today" sounds better than "Your order will be processed today." The first sounds more personal, whereas the latter, especially when used frequently, sounds unnecessarily formal.

24. Avoid using URGENT and IMPORTANT.

Even more so than the high-priority option, you must at all times try to avoid these types of words in an e-mail or subject line. Only use this if it is a really, really urgent or important message.

25. Avoid long sentences.

Try to keep your sentences to a maximum of 15-20 words. E-mail is meant to be a quick medium and requires a different kind of writing than letters. If a person receives an e-mail that looks like a dissertation, chances are that they will not even attempt to read it!

26. Don't send or forward e-mails containing libelous, defamatory, offensive, racist, or obscene remarks.

By sending or even just forwarding one libelous or offensive remark in an e-mail, you and your company can face court cases resulting in multi-million dollar penalties.

27. Don't forward virus hoaxes or schemes

If you receive an e-mail message warning you of a new unstoppable virus that will immediately delete everything from your computer, this is most probably a hoax. By forwarding hoaxes you use valuable bandwidth and sometimes virus hoaxes contain viruses themselves in an attached file that will supposedly stop the dangerous virus. The same goes for scheme letters that promise incredible riches or ask your help for a charitable cause. Even if the content seems to be bona fide, the senders are usually not. Since it is impossible to find out whether a letter like that is real or not, the best place for it is the trash.

28. Keep your language gender neutral.

In this day and age, avoid using sexist language such as: "The user should add a signature by configuring his e-mail program." Apart from using he/she, you can also use the neutral gender: "The user should add a signature by configuring the e-mail program."

29. Use the Cc: field sparingly.

Try not to use the Cc: field unless the recipient in the Cc: field knows why they are receiving a copy of the message. Using the Cc: field can be confusing since the recipients might not know who is supposed to act on the message. Also, when responding to a Cc: message, should you include the other recipient in the Cc: field as well? This will depend on the situation. In general, do not include the person in the Cc: field unless you have a particular reason for wanting this person to see your response.

Exercise 2 Pair up and answer the following questions.

1. It is a good idea to read your e-mail regularly, daily if possible.
   a. True
   b. False
2. It is a good idea to reply promptly to any e-mail you receive. Do not take a long time before you answer an e-mail.
   a. True
   b. False
3. You can assume that every e-mail you send will be read.
   a. True
   b. False
4. It is fine to send chain letters or to forward any such letters you receive.
   a. True
   b. False
5. It is always OK to send an e-mail to every person on a mailing list.
   a. True
   b. False
6. You should e-mail only people you know would want to receive your e-mail unless the message is of importance to every recipient.
   a. True
   b. False

7. Unless you are communicating with a close friend, you should include your e-mail signature at the end of each message.
   a. True
   b. False
8. A good e-mail rule is not to write anything you would not say in public.
   a. True
   b. False
9. It is OK to forward a personal e-mail without the original sender's knowledge or consent.
   a. True
   b. False
10. A person should not use e-mail to "flame." Flaming is aggressive and abusive language used to criticize others.
   a. True
   b. False
11. It is easy to stop an e-mail from being sent once you have clicked "Send."
   a. True
   b. False
12. It is fraudulent and illegal to pretend you are someone else when sending e-mail.
   a. True
   b. False
13. It is OK to make changes to an e-mail you receive and to pass it on to someone else without telling them where you have made changes.
   a. True
   b. False
14. E-mail must follow all laws that govern copyrights, defamation, discrimination, and other forms of written communication.
   a. True
   b. False
15. You should clean your inbox often and delete unwanted messages.
   a. True
   b. False
16. A good e-mail message will have the subject line blank.
   a. True
   b. False
17. It is a good idea to review your e-mail messages before sending them.
   a. True
   b. False
18. Most good e-mail systems have a spell checker, and it is a good idea to check your spelling.
   a. True
   b. False
19. When replying to an e-mail message, you should reply to all recipients of the original message.
   a. True
   b. False
20. Read all your e-mail, even if you do not know the sender.
   a. True
   b. False

Business Writing Simulation

Keeping in mind the e-mail etiquette rules on the previous pages, write a business e-mail requesting last year's sales figures.

To	Enter ',' to divide mail address when you send message more than one.	Address
Cc		Address
Bcc		Address
Subject		
Editor Type	◉ HTML Editor ◎ Word Editor ◎ Text Editor	

Source

Style | Format Normal | Font | Size 10pt

Unit 11 Writing Reports

Learning Objective:
After studying this unit, you should be able to....

- Learn to write clearly with a logical structure that is easy to follow.
- Understand how to write a business report that is concise and to the point.

Questionnaire : Knowing your readers and users

When writing a report, the first thing you will need to do is to consider your readers and their potential requirements.

You'll need to find out:

- Why is the report needed? (What are the real issues? How did they arise?)
- Who is going to use it?
- What are they hoping to get out of it?
- Are they looking for specific ideas or information or for a solution to a specific problem?
- What do they already know?
- What are their attitudes to the topic of the report?
- What decisions are likely to be made as a result of your report?

Activity

Pair up and discuss how a report should be structured.

Important points of a business report

- A report is typically divided into five areas:
  - **Terms of Reference** : This section gives background information on the reason for the report. It usually includes the person requesting the report.
  - **Procedure** : The procedure provides the exact steps taken and methods used for the report.
  - **Findings** : The findings point out discoveries made during the course of the report investigation.
  - **Conclusions** : The conclusions provide logical conclusions based on the findings.

- **Recommendations** : The recommendations state actions that the writer of the report feels need to be taken based on the findings and conclusions.

- Reports should be concise and factual. Opinions are given in the "Conclusions" section. However, these opinions should be based on facts presented in the "Findings" section.
- Use simple tenses (usually the simple present) to express facts.
- Use the imperative form (Discuss the possibility ..., Give priority ..., etc.) in the "Recommendations" section as these apply to the company as a whole.

Example Report

Employee Benefits Satisfaction Report

Terms of Reference

Margaret Anderson, Director of Personnel, requested this report on employee benefits satisfaction. The report was submitted to her by June 28th.

Procedure

A representative selection of 15% of all employees were interviewed in the period between April 1st and April 15th. concerning:

1. Overall satisfaction with our current benefits package
2. Problems encountered when dealing with the personnel department
3. Suggestions for the improvement of communication policies
4. Problems encountered when dealing with our HMO

Findings

1. Employees were generally satisfied with the current benefits package.
2. Some problems were encountered when requesting vacation due to what is perceived as long approval waiting periods.
3. Older employees repeatedly had problems with HMO prescription drugs procedures.
4. Employees between the ages of 22 and 30 reported few problems with our HMO.
5. Most employees complained about the lack of dental insurance in our benefits package.
6. The most common suggestion for improvement was for the ability to process benefits requests online.

Conclusions

1. Older employees, those over 50, are having serious problems with our HMO's ability to provide prescription drugs.
2. Our benefits request system needs to be revised as most complaints concern in-house processing.
3. Improvements need to be made in personnel department response time.
4. Information technology improvements should be considered as employees become more technologically savvy.

Recommendations

1. Meet with HMO representatives to discuss the serious nature of complaints concerning prescription drug benefits for older employees.
2. Give priority to vacation request response time as employees need faster approval in order to be able to plan their vacations.
3. Take no special actions for the benefits package of younger employees.
4. Discuss the possibility of adding an online benefits requests system to our company Intranet.

A signature and date below

1. Name
2. Date

General Structure of Business Reports

A committee or a person in authority usually asks for a report. Information on the method of inquiry that you used, what you found out, what it means, and possibly your recommendations will be required.

The recommended layout is one that is "tried and tested." It is formal, but if used properly, it helps you to write an efficient, clear report. The five areas of a business report, Terms of Reference, Procedure, Findings, Conclusions, and Recommendations, fall into four basic categories. The four categories are Introduction, Details, Response, and Close.

The **Introduction** is:

- Title (at the top of the report and often underlined)
- Terms of Reference
- Procedure

The **Details** are:
- Findings
- Conclusions

The **Response** is:
- Recommendations

The **Close** is:
- Signature
- Date

Here are some notes on what each of the sections should contain.

- *The title* needs to state briefly what the report is about.
- *The terms of reference* explain the purpose of the report, what exactly has been requested, who has asked for the report, and when it is to be handed in. If no date is mentioned then use any reasonable date. Often it will be "as soon as possible."
- *The procedure* lists and explains how the information was gathered.
- *The findings* are the facts clearly stated. Under "Findings" there should be *no opinions* on what has been found out.
- *The conclusions* are explanations of the findings and a discussion of what they mean to the firm of the person who asked for the report.
- *The recommendations* contain suggestions for future action.
- *The signature* is usually placed at the end of a report.
- *The date* is usually the one on which the report is written.

Here are notes on a few of the other possible structures.

A style often used for brief, formal reports can be:
- Introduction, which includes a title and a "Terms of Reference" statement
- Findings
- Conclusions
- Signature and Date

Another fairly common style, particularly for less formal reports, is
- Introduction
- Analysis
- Solution
- Signature and Date

There are other equally acceptable formats. All of them should help the clarity of all aspects of the report. There should be a sensible arrangement of ideas with linked conclusions and recommendations. There must be no confusion about what the findings are and what follows from them. The language in a report needs to be clear, easy to follow, neutral, and not emotional or excited.

Exercise 1-1 Jack Vasari works for Larsen, an American ice cream company. Read his report. Is the main topic:

A. a business trip? B. a new market? C. a new product?

JAPAN REPORT

Introduction
Earlier this month, I visited Japan to investigate the possibility of introducing our products there. Although Larsen is a leading ice cream producer in the United States, it is not well known in Japan.

The Market
The ice cream market in Japan is very competitive and is now open to foreign companies. Sales of regular and high-quality products have risen steadily in recent years (see attached sales figures). I visited wholesalers, retailers, and sales reps in the Tokyo and Osaka areas and also spoke to consumer focus groups. I discovered that Japanese consumers pay attention to:
a) flavor: lighter flavors are popular
b) image: effective advertising and attractive packaging are essential
c) ingredients: all ingredients must be pure and information should be provided on packaging
d) package / portion size: sizes are generally much smaller than in the U.S.
e) price: although we are not aiming for the lower-end market, prices should be no higher than those of our main competitors
f) etiquette: outside the home, Japanese consumers prefer to eat ice cream at the point of purchase; eating in the street is generally not acceptable, although this is changing.

Conclusion
Based on my research, I suggest that we first introduce a limited range of U.S.-made lines in retail stores. We should immediately investigate the possibility of production in Japan, and I recommend that we offer a number of ice cream café franchises in the Tokyo area as soon as possible.

Exercise 1-2 Write short answers to the questions.

a. Is Larsen well-known in Japan? ______________________________

b. Where did Jack go in Japan? ______________________________

c. Is the Japanese market growing? ______________________________

d. Are consumers only interested in flavor? ______________________________

e. Does Jack think Larsen should sell ice cream in Japan? ______________________________

Exercise 2 A report generally follows this sequence:

Title:	a short, clear explanation of what the report is about, found at the top of the report
Introduction:	a summary of the report
Findings:	the important facts
Conclusion:	the writer's opinions based on the facts in the body of the report

Read the sentences below. They are from two different reports. Which reports are they from? Write "1" or "2" beside each item. Then, next to each one write "T" (Title), "I" (Introduction), "F" (Findings), or "C" (Conclusion).

______ I recommend that we continue the program and encourage other hotels to do the same.

______ We found that the program cut laundry costs by up to 24% and improved our image among guests.

__1T__ Linsen Reuse Program: a Progress Report

______ I have now completed my inquiry into the poor sales of the V602 camcorder.

______ The Future of the V602 Camcorder

______ I present below an overview of the linen reuse program. Further details can be found in the attachment.

______ Based on my research, I strongly suggest that we replace the V602 model.

______ I found that 90% of consumers in our survey think that the V602 model is too large and too heavy.

Business Writing Simulation

Situation

You work for Snugdale Construction Limited, a large firm of building contractors, based at Papermill Road, Wolverhampton WV4 6EP. The administrative manager is Mrs. Ann Lister. The e-mail address is snugdale@wol.co.uk and the telephone numbers are 01902 336033/336044 and 01902 336055 (fax).

Question

Mrs. Lister has asked you to visit two of Snugdale's showhouses and to write a report on your findings. She is particularly interested in suggestions for improvements. You chose to look at two very similar houses, both detached homes costing £9,000: the Charlesdale house at Stafford and the Pennington house at Shrewsbury.

Here are your notes:

> Path leading to door (Charlesdale) – muddy and one of our own vehicles was parked on the front lawn.
>
> At the Pennington the door was closed. I rang the bell.
> NOT GOOD FOR POTENTIAL TRADE.
> (POSSIBLE BUYERS PUT OFF?)
>
> The outside (Pennington) was clean, but the garden was not weeded.
> Both furnished and decorated well – some mud on carpets (Charlesdale).
> At Charlesdale there was no manager on duty and help was not offered by anyone else.
> Pennington – no leaflets showing prices.

Write the letter.

Terms of Reference

Procedure

Findings

The showhouses were:

1.

2.

	PENNINGTON	CHARLESDALE
approach		
interior		
service		

Conclusions

▶

▶

Recommendations

Shrewsbury

♠

♠

♠

Stafford

♠

♠

♠

♠

♠

Unit 12 Writing Proposals

Learning Objective:
After studying this unit, you should be able to....

- Explain how to submit a proposal to persuade the company that you can do the job.
- Write a business letter that will win you an invitation to make a formal presentation or win you the contract outright.

Questionnaire : Twenty-five things to check before you submit

The development phrase

1. Have I analyzed the client's needs thoroughly and creatively?
2. Have I turned the statement of need into an overall strategy?
3. Have I checked my proposal for continuity and consistency?

Content

4. Is the creative strategy a good one?
5. Are the facts accurate?
6. Is the creative strategy supported by sufficient evidence and examples?
7. Is the proposed solution clearly worthwhile?
8. Is there any vagueness, abstraction, or generalization?
9. Is there too much detail and no overview or sense of perspective?
10. Is the proposal client-centered or us-centered?

Organization

11. Do the cover letter and executive summary attract the reader's interest?
12. Is the proposal one unified, persuasive argument? Is there one strategy to which everything is related?
13. Are the parts arranged in a coherent, logical order?
14. Is there closure to each major section?
15. Have I structured the information in a way that considers the reader's point of view?
16. Are my headings clear, properly worded, and parallel?
17. Is each section organized around (1) the client's need, (2) the solution, and (3) the supporting details?

Style

18. Are the sentences easy to understand?
19. Are all technical terms and jargon used correctly?

20. Have I avoided clichés?
21. Is the proposal concise?
22. Is the level of writing appropriate for the reader?

Accuracy

23. Are there mistakes in grammar, usage, spelling, or typing?
24. Are there mistakes in names, titles, dates, costs, or other details?
25. Is the proposal neat, professional, and easy to read?

Activity

Pair up and talk about the key factors of a business proposal and make a list of them.

What is a Business Proposal?

Unlike a business plan, which is written to run your company and raise capital, a business proposal is an unsolicited or solicited bid for business. There are two types of business proposals that can help you gain more business to grow your company.

Solicited Business Proposal: A corporation or government body is seeking a business to fulfill a project or complete a task. It allows companies to bid for the project. An open bid is placed on the market with other companies competing for an interview spot. The winning candidate is offered the project.

Unsolicited Business Proposal: At some point, your small business may want to do business with a larger company or forge a joint venture. A well-written business proposal can win the hearts and minds of your target audience. If you need to write a business proposal to win a bid, you will need to know the key winning elements of a successful proposal. Make sure your proposal stands out in the stack of competitor proposals by including the following 5 elements:

5 Key Elements of Winning Business Proposals

- **Solutions:** After you have written a lead paragraph on the company's needs and problems, follow up with a solid presentation of how your business can provide solutions. The key here is to promise solutions you can deliver.
- **Benefits:** All winning business proposals clearly outline for the company the benefits to be gained from doing business with you. If your small business can offer complete confidentiality and meet tight deadlines, state it in your benefits section.
- **Credibility:** This is often the overlooked portion of a business proposal, but all winning proposals glow with credibility. If you have worked with clients in the same field or have an award-winning business, then third-party endorsements will build credibility.

- **Samples:** A business proposal with samples and evidence of your ability to deliver is vital to gaining the winning bid. A small sample of your work can show your ability to do the job.
- **Targeted Audience:** A winning business proposal is all about communication. Speak in a language spoken by your intended audience. If the proposal evaluators are from an engineering background or financial department, use the appropriate jargon.

Business Proposal Dilemma

Business proposals form the lifeline of commerce for many small companies and consultants. Responding to a request for proposal (RFP) from a potential buyer can result in capturing more business or becoming drained on time and cash resources. Every entrepreneur must decide whether or not to pursue the opportunity with a business proposal. Learn what you need to consider before you delve in and respond to an RFP.

Making the decision to bid on a RFP is a critical one. The RFP process can be beneficial to all parties involved by providing clear expectations of the project and reducing risks. However, if you lose the bid, absorb the loss and move on. It is far better to do some early analysis and look at your potential. Consider these 8 points to help you determine whether to respond to an RFP.

Determine the Budget: Before you make the decision to submit a business proposal, assess the size and scope of the bidding project. Find out how much the contract will be worth. Weigh the time and costs of submitting a business proposal against the revenue gain and term of the contract.

Assess the Competition: The size of the bidding pool will have a direct result on your closure rate. An open bid on the Internet with hundreds of competing companies can be less attractive than a ten company competition in your own backyard. Play the better odds.

Review Administrative Information: Bidders on an RFP will be best served by reviewing the administrative information of the buying company's bid information. This information will often lay out the guidelines to submit a successful bid. Be suspicious of vague information.

"For perceptive suppliers, lack of instructions may signal a weak RFP team and a confused or conflicted project. This potential weakness may influence whether they decide to continue with their proposal," says Bud Porter-Roth in "Request for Proposal: A Guide to Effective RFP Development."

Bid Implications: Look closely at the prospect of winning the bid. Will the project add to your portfolio? Will you be able to leverage this contract into more business in the future?

Match Skills: Every project will require specific skills for execution. Before you decide to develop a business proposal, look at the skill set of your small business. Can you realistically meet the needs of the buying organization?

Request for Information: At times companies will be reviewing products or services in the marketplace for a project. These organizations are not taking bids at this stage and could be using the request to insure their current supplier stays competitive.

Set Your Qualifications: Instead of responding to all RFPs in your marketplace, it is more prudent to determine what sort of projects and companies you want to work with. Does this particular client match your target market?

RFP Timing: Consider the length of time required to write a business proposal. Building a winning proposal is more than "cutting and pasting" data to convince the company to hire you. Don't forget to look at your own timetable and avoid overcommitting.

Winning the business proposal game means looking carefully at your options and assessing the risks. Remember your time is far more limited than most buying companies. Respect it and business success can be yours.

Exercise 1 Complete the quiz below and check the answers.

1. Business proposals need to provide more than just attractive ideas--readers look for evidence of practical, achievable solutions.
   a. True
   b. False
2. In an unsolicited proposal, your introduction does NOT need to convince readers that a problem or opportunity exists.
   a. True
   b. False
3. Transitions connect ideas by helping readers move from one thought to the next.
   a. True
   b. False
4. "Previews" help readers prepare for upcoming information and "reviews" help them verify and clarify what they have just read.
   a. True
   b. False
5. Which of the following should you provide in your proposal?
   a. "You" attitude
   b. Demonstration of your knowledge
   c. Information and examples
   d. All of the above
6. Which of the following does NOT belong in the introduction of a proposal?
   a. Statement of problem
   b. Scope
   c. Work plan
   d. Solution
7. Which of the following belongs in the body of a proposal?
   a. Proposal approach
   b. Costs
   c. Statement of qualifications
   d. All of the above

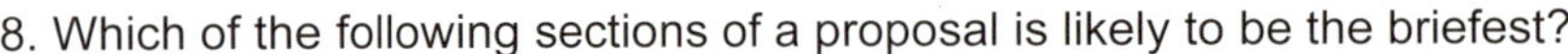

8. Which of the following sections of a proposal is likely to be the briefest?
   a. Introduction
   b. Closing
   c. Body
   d. None of the above
9. Which of the following descriptions applies to review sections?
   a. Cue readers about the content that follows
   b. Tie ideas together and show their connections
   c. Help readers get ready for new information
   d. Help readers absorb details while keeping track of the big picture
10. Which of the following technological tools can help you create your reports and proposals?
    a. Templates
    b. Multimedia documents
    c. Linked documents
    d. All of the above

Business Writing Simulation

Write a business proposal or rewrite one you have created previously according to the following form.

Title:

Solutions:

Benefits:

Credibility:

Samples:

Targeted Audience:

Memo

Answer Key

Effective Business Writing Before you begin, take a minute to assess your writing style. You may discover that you know a lot more than you think, or you may discover specific areas where you need to improve. Either way, this exercise will help you assess your writing ability. Read each statement and mark the response.

Answer Key

| Unit 1 |

Exercise 1-1

a. *The computer that is in the hallway is brand new.* (The writer identifies one particular computer "in the hallway" rather than the computer that is somewhere else. The location is essential to the sentence)

b. *The computer, which is in the hallway, is brand new.* (The writer assumes there is only one computer and adds only descriptive information-"in the hallway" is nonessential to the meaning of the sentence.

Exercise 1-2

1. He bought his first car last fall. It never ran well.
2. He bought his first car last fall, but it never ran well.
3. He bought his first car last fall; it never ran well.

Exercise 2

a. I thought I had completed the project; consequently, I was surprised to hear about the additional work.

b. We have prepared your estimate; however, you should sign it by Friday.

c. The partners' retreat will be held in March; therefore, all business matters will be discussed then.

Exercise 3

1. The executive watched the competition, but the competition went ahead with the takeover.
2. During our meeting she was gracious but shrewd.
3. Today more women are becoming executives in corporations.
4. The job was difficult; therefore, he quit.
   OR: The job was difficult. Therefore, he quit.
5. My suitcase contained files, pencils, books, and paper.
6. We thought we would have to work late; therefore, we were happy to be home before dark.
   OR: We thought we would have to work late. Therefore, we were happy to be home before dark.
7. My boss's car was in the shop; consequently, she borrowed her husband's.
8. In preparation for the meeting, Mr. Jones asked us to do three things: set up the equipment, dust the tables, and empty the ashtrays.
9. We wanted to go to the partners' meeting, but we were unable to leave before the weekend.
10. Lois's résumé arrived yesterday; moreover, she phoned for an interview next week.

Exercise 4

Southwestern Corporation
333 LaSalle Street
Chicago, IL 60610

March 29, 20xx

Mr. John C. Fremont
2929 East Sycamore Street
Chicago, IL 60601

Dear Mr. Fremont:

Thank you for meeting with us and for your time and effort in preparing for the interview. We appreciate your accommodating us with a flexible schedule.

We are in the final stages of processing your application, and we need three more items for our files: your social security number, permanent home address, and your date of birth. As soon as we get this information, we can proceed to complete your permanent records.

Everyone here at Southwestern Corporation is looking forward to working with you, and we are eager to have you begin as soon as possible. Please call me as soon as you can with this information.

Sincerely,

Janet L. Estes
Senior Vice President

Exercise 5

Spelling:
unfortuneatly → unfortunately
iterinary → itinerary

Punctuation:
We would like, to invite... → We would like to invite... (remove comma)
... Conference, I will make... → ...Conference. I will make... (change comma to period)

Capitalization:
california → California
mexican → Mexican

Verb tenses:
contacting → contact
looked → look

Prepositions:
during two days → for two days
flying in → flying to

Writing Simulation

Exercise 1-1

to introduce himself

Exercise 1-2

a. F b. F c. T d. T e. F

Exercise 1-3

a. short
b. joined
c. previously
d. customers
e. doing business with
f. queries
g. do not hesitate to
h. contact

Exercise 1-4

1. brief
2. replaced
3. marketing
4. Cosmetics
5. September
6. started working for
7. three years ago
8. before
9. representative
10. clients
11. working
12. questions
13. free
14. touch

| Unit 2 |

Exercise 1

1. We are sponsoring a company picnic next month in Lincoln Grove. If you need directions, please contact us.
2. Currently we have no job openings. Thank you.
3. Before you leave, please turn off the lights.
4. At their meeting, the board will consider our increase in salary.

Exercise 2

1. It was both a long and very tedious meeting.
2. Joe likes a job with challenging and stimulating work. OR
   Joe likes a job that challenges him and that keeps him stimulated.
3. Poor writing wastes time, costs money, and alienates customers.
4. [No change needed]
5. [No change needed]

Writing Simulation

Exercise 1-1

a. Because he wants to change the arrangements for the meeting.
b. Yes, she can.

Exercise 1-2 Possible answers

A Dear Ms. Kapoor,

I'm afraid I have to change my plans for next week and it's not possible for me to meet with you on Wednesday. I wonder if we could reschedule it for 11 a.m. Friday?

I'm very sorry about the inconvenience.

Best regards / wishes,
Jeff Roussos

B Dear Mr. Roussos,

It's no inconvenience at all. 11 a.m. Friday is fine with me.

Best wishes / regards,
Karishma Kapoor

| Unit 3 |

Exercise 1

1. Body 2. Inside address 3. Heading or Letterhead 4. Signature 5. Enclosure

Exercise 2-2

a. EBA Business
b. She is writing to a company and she does not know the name of the person she is writing to.
c. *Business World* magazine
d. She wants the company to send her a copy of their latest catalog.

Exercise 2-3

May 2, 2005

RBM Manufacturing Company, Inc.
11295 9th Avenue
New York, New York 10055

Dear Sir or Madam:

We intend to purchase a new laser printer/copier before the end of the fiscal year. We would like to consider an RBM copier.

We run approximately 3000 copies a month and prefer a machine with fax capability. We would like a collator, but rarely need to run off more than 25 copies at any one time.

We would also like to know about your warranty and repair service.

Since our fiscal year ends June 30, 2005, we hope to hear from you soon.

Sincerely yours,

William Wilson

William Wilson
Office Manager

Writing Simulation

Crescent Finance Company

Telephone 870 3269

71-75 Langan Road
Dublin 11

(date)
Mrs. Maeve Nolan
Manager
Shamrock Bank
Springfield Road
Bishopstown
Cork

Dear Mrs. Nolan:

Mr. Sunil Cheema (dob March 15, 1970)

Mr. Cheema worked at Crescent Finance from September 1994 until August 1997. Following an introductory period sampling the work of each of our departments he was appointed to the Sales Support staff.

His attendance and punctuality were excellent and he displayed a high level of intelligence to complement his likeable personality.

During his time with us he was always diligent and interested in furthering his knowledge through participating in a number of training courses. He left Crescent Finance in order to study Information Technology and Accounts at Cork University.

I wish him well and consider him suited to working in your Accounts Department. We thought sufficiently highly of him to have offered him promotion.

Yours sincerely

Colette Doherty (Mrs)
Proprietor

| Unit 4 |

Exercise 1

a. We must sell our surplus products. (6)
b. We prepared this instruction manual to help our dealers serve their customers. (12)
c. The collision destroyed the duplicator. (5)
d. Page four of the enclosed pamphlet shows further construction details. (10)

Exercise 2-1

1.c 2.e 3.b 4.f 5.a 6.d

Exercise 2-2

a. speedy b. sudden c. position
d. well e. address f. sure

Exercise 3

a. Congratulations on your promotion!
b. Please accept my congratulations on the opening of your branch in Milan.
c. I would like to congratulate you on your twentieth year of employment with the company.

Exercise 4

1. writing 2. on 3. as
4. will 5. co-operation 6. companies

Exercise 5

A
1. I hope you get well soon.
2. Just concentrate on getting better.

B
1. my sincerest sympathy at this difficult time.
2. if there is anything I can do to help.

Writing Example

MEMORANDUM

TO: All Employees
FROM: The President
DATE: September 15, 20xx
RE: Staff Meeting Postponement

To help get our sales volume back on track, we are postponing our staff meeting until early winter. We will let you know our meeting's new date as soon as we select it.

I appreciate your extra efforts and encourage you to be productive and work to increase sales during the 4th quarter.

| Unit 5 |

Exercise 1

The system may automatically shut down if any installation errors occur.

Exercise 2

But:
Connie Green performed the job well.
To Whom it May Concern:
Students must provide their own lab jackets. OR:
Each student must provide his or her own lab jacket.

Exercise 3

Your order will be available in two weeks.

Exercise 4 - Example

Thank you for offering me the position as General Manager at Simon's Inc. I appreciate your prompt and generous offer. Unfortunately, I am unable to accept the position. I have accepted a different position that will allow me to utilize my communication and customer-service skills.

| Unit 6 |

Exercise 1-1

b

Exercise 1-2

a. because she doesn't know the name/no name was given in the advertisement
b. Plastics Monthly
c. high quality plastic household goods
d. their latest catalogue, a full price list, and details of discounts

Exercise 2

1. Appreciation and apology
2. Ms. Klein
3. To thank Klein for her order and to apologize for the delay

Writing Example

Snugdale Construction Limited

Mr. Frank Timmins
17 New Street
Wolverhampton
WV6 8RS

RE: Newlands Farm Site

Dear Mr. Timmins :

Thank you for your letter of April 12 drawing our attention to the problems you are experiencing.
I shall be contacting you very soon to arrange a meeting to discuss in detail what we can do to alleviate any nuisance.

Certainly we will not tolerate any rudeness to existing residents and we are issuing a memo to that effect to all our employees.
We intend to replace your fence as soon as building

work is finished. Meanwhile, should you have any further problem prior to our meeting please let me know directly.

Sincerely,

Ann Lister
Administrative Manager

| Unit 7 |

Exercise 1-1 Possible answers

a. I am writing to complain about your latest shipment.
b. I am writing about a problem with the installation of computer network software.
c. I am writing in reference to order # XJ 4311.
d. I am writing to complain about the redecoration of our corporate headquarters.

Exercise 1-2 Possible answers

a. I am writing to complain about your latest shipment, which was delivered this morning.
b. I am writing about a problem with the installation of computer network software, which was completed last week.
c. I am writing in reference to order # XJ 4311, which arrived on Friday.
d. I am writing to complain about the redecoration of our corporate headquarters, which was finished yesterday.

Exercise 2 Possible answers

a. We regret to inform you that the shipment arrived late. The promised delivery date was January 22, but it arrived February 6. Please find enclosed a copy of the shipping order.
b. Unfortunately, you sent us the wrong model. We ordered TS400 models, but we received TS300. I am attaching a photocopy of the order.
c. I am sorry to say that the work was unsatisfactory. There are cracks in the walls. Please find enclosed photographs of the work.

Exercise 3-1

a. items
b. ensure
c. replacement
d. inspect

Exercise 3-2 Possible answers

Note to Teachers: On the board, write the headings "Problems" and "Solutions." Ask students to tell you what each problem was in Exercise 2 and write them on the board.

Problem : The goods were damaged.
Solution : Please send us the replacement goods as soon as possible.

Problem : The shipment arrived late.
Solution : Please insure that future shipments arrive on time.

Problem : You sent us the wrong model.
Solution : Please send us the correct items by January 14.

Problem : The work was unsatisfactory.
Solution : Please send someone to inspect the building immediately.

Exercise 4-1

a. Thank
b. Refer
c. Give
d. Say
e. Write

Answer Key

Exercise 4-2

Dear Mr. Watanabe,

1. Thank you for your letter dated October 26 concerning your recent order.
2. We are sorry to hear that you received the wrong order.
3. Apparently, this was caused by a processing error.
4. We will send you the correct items free of charge.
5. Once again, please accept our apologies for the inconvenience, and we look forward to serving you again in the future.

Sincerely,
Vince Picardo

Exercise 4-3

a. concerning
b. we are sorry to hear
c. this was caused by
d. free of charge
e. please accept our apologies

Exercise 4-4 Possible answer

Dear Ms. Pang:

Thank you for your e-mail dated/of May 10 concerning the installation of computer accounting software.

We regret to learn that the installation was unsatisfactory. Apparently, this was the result of a fault in the CD. We will send a replacement CD immediately at no extra cost.

Once again, we would like to apologize for the inconvenience, and we look forward to serving you again in the future.

Sincerely,
(student's name)

| Unit 8 |

Exercise 1

Headline, Offer, Proof, Action, Postscript

| Unit 9 |

Activity

1.False 2.False 3.False 4.False
5.False

Exercise 1

1.C	2.D	3.D	4.A	5.C
6.A	7.C	8.B	9.D	10.C

Exercise 2

·Subject line
: Span Screening @ MIT - auto purging extended to 21 days
·Who (target audience)
: spamscreen-users@mit.edu
·Purpose
: to alert users to an upcoming change in service
·Background
: e-mail accounts previous set to auto-purge messages older than 14 days from "Spamscreen" folder on the MIT mail system
·What
: Change in Spamscreen folder auto-purge
·When / by when (deadlines)
: changes to occur by October 4th, 2004
·Why (purpose)
: to prepare for another important upcoming enhancement in their service
·Benefits (to target audience)
: allows additional time for new MIT colleagues and

students to acclimate to the new environment and this important service

·Action requested

: visit the website or contact the Help Desk with comments, suggestions, or questions, if desired

·Signature block

: Theresa M. Regan

| Unit 10 |

Exercise 1

Revised Lead

Tim, Gloria, and I agree our association faces enormous challenges. Let's hold a strategic planning session by December to review board members' concerns and begin planning for the future.

Exercise 2

1. True	2. True	3. False	4. False
5. False	6. False	7. True	8. True
9. False	10. True	11. False	12. True
13. False	14. True	15. True	16. False
17. True	18. True	19. False	20. False

| Unit 11 |

Exercise 1-1

b

Exercise 1-2

a. No, it is not.
b. to the Tokyo and Osaka areas
c. Yes, it is.
d. No, they are not.
e. Yes, he does.

Exercise 2

1C , 1F, 2I, 2T, 1I, 2C, 2F

* See example of Unit 11 Writing Simulation on page 106

| Unit 12 |

1. a) True
2. b) False
3. a) True
4. a) True
5. d) All of the above
6. d) Solution
7. d) All of the above
8. a) Introduction
9. d) Helps readers absorb details while keeping track of the big picture
10. d) All of the above

Unit 11 | Writing Simulation

Terms of Reference

A report has been requested by Mrs. Lister on a visit to two of our showhouses. The report is to be ready as soon as possible.

Procedure

I made unannounded visits to 2 different sites.

Findings

The showhouses were:

1. Pennington sited at Shrewsbury
2. Charlesdale sited at Stafford

Both are very similar detached homes selling at £90,000.

	PENNINGTON	CHARLESDALE
approach	weeds in garden otherwise clean appearance	muddy path Snugdale vehicle on lawn
interior	well-furnished and decorated	well furnished and decorated mud on carpets
service	door closed no price-list	no duty manager available no help offered

Conclusions

- ► Neither site met our high showhouse
- ► Closed door and lack of help are unacceptable

Recommendations

Shrewsbury

- ♠ Ready access to showhouse
- ♠ Availability of leaflets and price-lists
- ♠ Tidy garden

Stafford

- ♠ Duty rotation for staff
- ♠ Staff training check
- ♠ Clean carpets
- ♠ Paths cleared
- ♠ Specified areas for parking